MW01099151

EVERYDAY POWERFOODS

TRIPLE TESTED

THE AUSTRALIAN WOMEN'S WEEKLY · TEST KITCHEN

THE AUSTRALIAN
Women's Weekly

EVERYDAY
POWERFOODS

THE AUSTRALIAN WOMEN'S WEEKLY
TRIPLE TESTED
TEST KITCHEN

CONTENTS

EVERYDAY
HEALTHY

WE LEAD SUCH BUSY LIVES WITH WORK AND FAMILY, THAT IT'S ALL TOO COMMON FOR WOMEN TO THINK ABOUT EVERYONE ELSE'S WELLBEING AHEAD OF THEIR OWN. HOW ARE YOU LOOKING AFTER YOURSELF?

A GOOD DIET IS A GREAT START

What we eat has a direct impact on the way in which we function and how we look. This is incredibly powerful because it means we have a certain amount of control over our health by what we choose to put into our body. A healthy diet packed full of fresh fruit and vegetables, lean proteins, wholegrains and healthy fats, regular activity and drinking plenty of water can regulate our energy levels and mood. It can help us to manage stress, improve digestion, maintain a healthy weight, improve fertility, nourish a growing baby, ease the symptoms of PMS and menopause and reduce the risk of some major chronic diseases. It can also help us to glow from the inside out.

GET OUTSIDE

Getting outside when the sun is shining and it's a beautiful day has very specific health benefits. It can provide us with precious vitamin D that we absorb on our skin from safe levels of sun exposure. When we're outside it also means we're more likely to be moving and active, breathing in fresh air and taking in the scenery which is fantastic for our physical and mental health.

QUICK WAYS TO RECHARGE

1 MINUTE *Switch off*
Turn off electronic devices at night as they can make it difficult to wind down and their light can disrupt our sleep patterns.

5 MINUTES *Breathe*
Close your eyes and take a big, long deep breath in, and gently let it out again, then repeat. This dampens our stress and allows our body to relax.

15 MINUTES *Walk*
It can be a slow amble or a brisk, cracking powerwalk – either way, getting up and moving can help release mood enhancing endorphins and give us time to clear our head.

30 MINUTES *Meditate*
Meditation is simply about emptying your mind of worries and cares. There are many ways to meditate, from classes or Apps to reading or gardening.

HAPPY HEALTHY MUMS

EAT TO NOURISH

It's common for women to put effort into their kid's meals and forget to properly nourish themselves. As busy women, what we eat couldn't be more important, from pre-conception right through to juggling the demands of a family; it's a time when we have very specific nutritional needs.

WHEN YOU'RE LACKING IN...

Iron Iron deficiency is the most common nutritional deficiency, particularly among young women. Iron is used to carry oxygen around the blood so low iron can make us feel lethargic, weak, dizzy and short of breath. Iron is found in meat, legumes, fish and green leafy vegetables.

Zinc Needed for growth and development, a strong immune system and wound healing; a deficiency can impair immune function. Zinc is found in animal foods as well as nuts, wholegrains and legumes.

Vitamin B12 Is used to create red blood cells, nerves and DNA and a deficiency can make us feel very tired and lethargic. Vitamin B12 can only be found in animal products.

Calcium Builds bones and teeth. Deficiencies tend to present later in life when bones become brittle (osteoporosis). The best sources of calcium are dairy and a calcium-fortified foods like non-dairy milks.

Iodine Vital for producing thyroid hormones, which is associated with metabolism and bone maintenance. The best sources of iodine are seaweed, fish, dairy and eggs.

WOMEN'S HEALTH & EATING ORGANIC

Organic food has been grown without chemical herbicides and pesticides, and animals reared without synthetic hormones or antibiotics. There's no doubt that choosing some foods that are organic is worth it, especially for pregnant women and babies. Eating organic may reduce our exposure to potentially harmful chemicals, improve the nutritional value of that food and be tastier. How organic you go may be based on your budget and what foods you consume on a regular basis as to what you choose to eat organic.

PAMPER YOURSELF

Taking the time to pamper yourself is incredibly important so we can be the best version of ourselves. An easy, inexpensive way is to use products you've already got in your kitchen such as coconut oil for deep hair treatments and cucumber for a face mask. Food can be not only good for you on the inside, but on the outside as well.

Jaime Rose Chambers
ACCREDITED PRACTISING DIETITIAN & NUTRITIONIST
www.jaimerosenutrition.com.au

NUTRIENTS & THEIR FUNCTION

INGREDIENT	RICH IN	GOOD FOR
ALMONDS	VITAMIN H (BIOTIN)	Metabolises protein, fat and carbohydrate
AVOCADO	VITAMIN B5 (PANTOTHENIC ACID)	Energy, metabolism
BANANAS	POTASSIUM	Maintains normal heart function
BEETROOT	FOLATE	Prevent neural tube defects
BLUEBERRIES	ANTHOCYANINS	Enhances memory
CACAO	POLYPHENOLS	Blood sugar regulation
CAULIFLOWER	VITAMIN C	Reduces oxidative stress
CHERRIES	ANTHOCYANINS	Osteoarthritis relief
CHIA SEEDS	OMEGA 3 FATTY ACIDS (DHA)	Brain development
CHICKPEAS	INSOLUBLE FIBRE	Bowel function support
EGGS	CHOLINE	Nervous system signalling
GARLIC	ALLICIN	Antimicrobial properties
GREEK YOGHURT	CALCIUM	Builds and strengthens bones
KUMARA (Orange sweet potato)	BETA-CAROTENE	Eye health
LINSEEDS (flaxseeds)	OMEGA 3 FATTY ACIDS (ALA)	Protects blood vessels from inflammation
MUSHROOMS	SELENIUM	Healthy thyroid function
ORANGES	VITAMIN C	Skin anti-ageing
PEARS	FLAVONOIDS	Improves insulin sensitivity
POMEGRANATE	PUNICALAGINS	Potent antioxidant activity
QUINOA	MANGANESE	Skin integrity
SEAWEED (nori)	IODINE	Normal thyroid function and metabolism
SESAME SEEDS (tahini)	MAGNESIUM	Muscle relaxation
SPINACH	IRON	Blood production and transporting oxygen

JUICES AND SMOOTHIES

KALE &
BANANA
SMOOTHIE

PREP TIME **5 MINUTES** SERVES **4 (MAKES 1 LITRE)**

2 MEDIUM RIPE BANANAS (400G)
2 CUPS (60G) SHREDDED KALE LEAVES
1 MEDIUM AVOCADO (250G), CHOPPED COARSELY
1½ TABLESPOONS HONEY
2 CUPS (500ML) WATER
2 TEASPOONS LINSEEDS
CRUSHED ICE, TO SERVE

1 Place banana, kale, avocado, honey, the water and linseeds in a high-powdered juice blender; blend until smooth.
2 Pour smoothie into glasses filled with crushed ice. Serve immediately.

nutritional count per serving
10.2g total fat (2.1g saturated fat); 804kJ (192 cal); 21.7g carbohydrate; 2.4g protein; 3.5g fibre

tips Wash the kale leaves well and remove the stems before shredding. For a creamier textured smoothie, use frozen ripe bananas and make sure all the ingredients are cold.

ELECTROLYTE BOOSTER

PREP TIME **10 MINUTES** SERVES **2 (MAKES 1 LITRE)**

Blend 2 cups coconut water, 400g (12½oz) frozen
pineapple, 1 small (200g) avocado, ½ trimmed, chopped
baby (65g) fennel, ½ cup fresh mint leaves, 2 cups firmly
packed baby spinach and 2 tablespoons lime juice in a
high-speed blender until smooth. Serve over ice.

*tip Frozen pineapple is available from
supermarkets or you can freeze your own
portioned, peeled, cored and chopped
pineapple in zip-top bags.*

JUST LIKE A CHOCOLATE THICK SHAKE...

PREP TIME **10 MINUTES** SERVES **2 (MAKES 1 LITRE)**

Blend 2 cups unsweetened almond milk, 2 ripe medium
(260g) chopped frozen bananas, 1 small (200g) chopped
avocado, 1 cup firmly packed baby spinach, 2 tablespoons
cacao powder, ⅓ cup vanilla bean whey protein powder
(optional) or yoghurt and 1 tablespoon raw honey in a
high-speed blender until smooth. Serve over ice,
dusted with ¼ teaspoon extra cacao powder.

*tip Keep chopped ripe bananas in a zip-top bag
in the freezer to always have on hand.*

QUENCH YOUR THIRST

PICK ME-UP

BERRY BERRY LUSCIOUS

PREP TIME **10 MINUTES**   SERVES **2 (MAKES 3 CUPS)**

Soak 2 tablespoons of goji berries in 1 cup chilled coconut milk blend (see tip) for 10 minutes in a small bowl. Transfer to a high-speed blender; add 2 cups frozen mixed berries, 1 cup firmly packed baby spinach and another 1 cup chilled coconut milk blend. Blend until smooth. Serve over ice, topped with 1 tablespoon each goji berries and mixed berries.

tips We used Pureharvest Coco Quench a blend of coconut and rice milks; it has a thinner consistency than canned coconut milk, but still has a great coconut milk taste. The berries in this recipe pack some serious antioxidant punch.

GREEN TEA & KIWI SIPPER

PREP TIME **10 MINUTES (+ COOLING)**   SERVES **2**

Brew 2 green tea bags in 2 cups boiling water for 5 minutes. Discard tea bags. Stir in 1 tablespoon raw honey. Cool in the fridge. Place cooled tea in a high-speed blender with 1 cup frozen green grapes, 2 medium (170g) peeled chopped kiwifruits, 1 cup fresh mint leaves and 1 cup firmly packed baby spinach until smooth. Serve immediately over ice.

tips This drink separates quickly, so it is best made just before serving. Kiwifruit contains loads of fibre, vitamins C & E, antioxidants and minerals – zinc, calcium, iron, magnesium, copper and potassium. Kiwifruit are great for keeping skin, hair and nails glowing, healthy and strong.

HEALTHY HEART

GUT HEALTH

SPICED APPLE PIE
OAT SMOOTHIE

PREP TIME **5 MINUTES**   SERVES **2 (MAKES 1 LITRE)**

As well as being a great afternoon pick-me-up, you can pour the smoothie into a large glass bottle and take to work for a breakfast on the go.

1 VANILLA BEAN

1 CUP (90G) ROLLED OATS

2 TABLESPOON MACA POWDER (SEE TIPS)

1 CUP (250ML) ALMOND MILK

1 CUP (250ML) PURE APPLE JUICE

2 SMALL RED APPLES (260G), CORED, CHOPPED COARSELY

¼ CUP (70G) GREEK-STYLE YOGHURT

4 FRESH MEDJOOL DATES (20G), PITTED, CHOPPED COARSELY

1 TEASPOON GROUND CINNAMON

¼ TEASPOON GROUND NUTMEG

6 ICE CUBES

1 Split vanilla bean lengthways; scrape the seeds into a blender. Add remaining ingredients; blend until smooth.

2 Pour smoothie into tall glasses; sprinkle with a little extra ground cinnamon, if you like.

nutritional count per serving
19.9g total fat (3g saturated fat); 2174kJ (520 cal); 68.2g carbohydrate; 13.1g protein; 9g fibre

tips Maca powder is available from major supermarkets and health food stores. Maca is the root of a plant native to South America, where it has been consumed for several thousand years. It is a rich source of vitamin C, iron, copper and calcium, and a very good source of riboflavin, niacin, vitamin B6, potassium and manganese. It also contains about 14% protein and provides a good dose of fibre. Medjool dates are available from the fresh food section of major supermarkets. When pears are in season, use a juicy variety such as packham instead of the red apples and pear juice instead of apple juice.

TROPICAL
JUICE

PREP TIME **10 MINUTES** SERVES **2 (MAKES 2 CUPS)**

150G (4½ OUNCES) PAPAYA
150G (4½ OUNCES) PEELED FRESH PINEAPPLE
80G (2½ OUNCES) FROZEN MANGO
½ CUP (125ML) COCONUT WATER
½ CUP (125ML) POMEGRANATE JUICE
1 CUP ICE-CUBES
1 TABLESPOON TOASTED SHAVED COCONUT
1 TEASPOON POMEGRANATE SEEDS (SEE TIPS)

1 Place papaya, pineapple, mango, coconut water, pomegranate juice and ice-cubes in a high-powdered juice blender; blend until smooth.
2 Pour into glasses; top with shaved coconut and pomegranate seeds.

nutritional count per serving
2.4g total fat (1.7g saturated fat); 627kJ (150 cal); 28.1g carbohydrate; 2g protein; 4.7g fibre

tips *Fresh pomegranate seeds can sometimes be found in the fridge section of supermarkets and good greengrocers. To remove the seeds from a pomegranate, cut the fruit in half crossways; hold it, cut-side down, in the palm of your hand over a bowl, then hit the outside firmly with a wooden spoon. The seeds should fall out easily; discard any white pith that falls out with them. Pomegranate seeds will keep in the fridge for up to a week.*

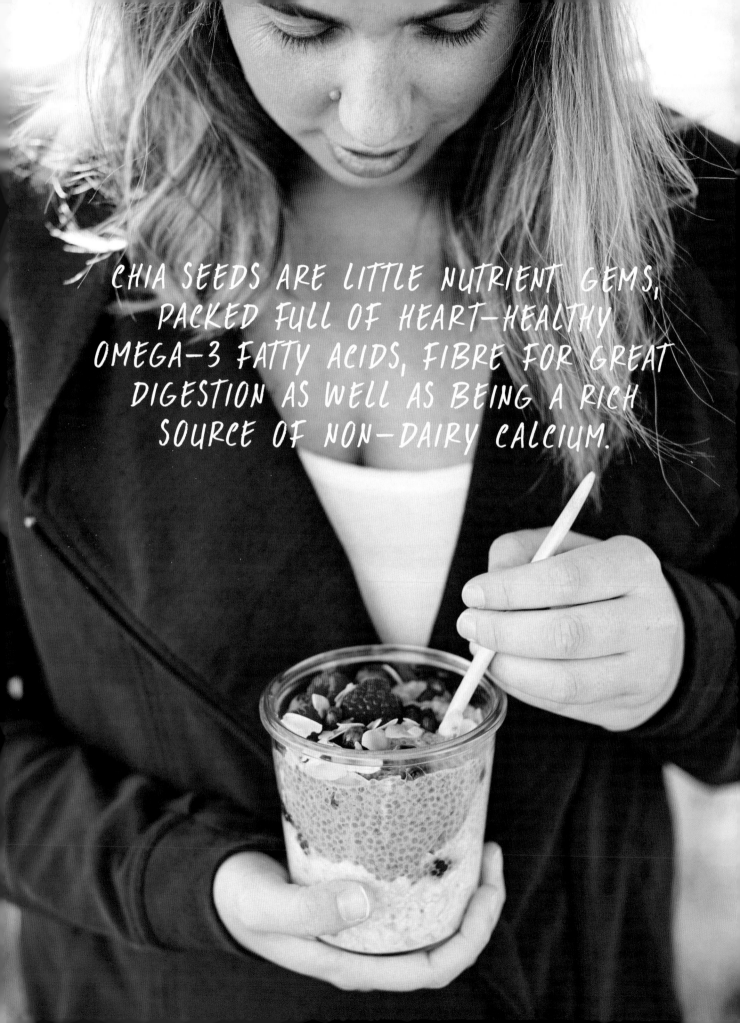

CHIA SEEDS ARE LITTLE NUTRIENT GEMS, PACKED FULL OF HEART-HEALTHY OMEGA-3 FATTY ACIDS, FIBRE FOR GREAT DIGESTION AS WELL AS BEING A RICH SOURCE OF NON-DAIRY CALCIUM.

CUCUMBER ICED GREEN TEA

PREP TIME **5 MINUTES (+ REFRIGERATION)**

MAKES **1 LITRE (4 CUPS)**

Brew 2 green tea bags in 3½ cups boiling water for 5 minutes. Stir in 1 tablespoon honey until dissolved. Cool in the fridge. Half fill a large jug with ice, then add ½ cup cucumber juice (see tips), 1 tablespoon lime juice, ½ cup crushed fresh mint leaves, 1 thinly sliced (130g) lebanese cucumber, ½ thinly sliced (75g) pink lady apple and the chilled green tea; stir to combine.

tips You will need to juice 2 medium (260g) lebanese cucumbers for the amount of juice required. If you don't have a juicer, use a blender; strain mixture through a fine sieve.

ALMOND CHAI TEA

PREP + COOK TIME **25 MINUTES (+ REFRIGERATION)**

MAKES **1.25 LITRES (5 CUPS)**

Place 3 cups water in a large saucepan with 2 teaspoons black tea leaves, 2 cinnamon sticks, 1 vanilla bean split lengthways, 1 tablespoon raw honey, 5 thick slices ginger, 6 cloves, 8 bruised cardamon pods, ½ teaspoon black peppercorns and 3 x 5cm (2-inch) strips orange rind; bring to the boil. Reduce heat; simmer for 20 minutes or until reduced to 1 cup. Remove from heat; refrigerate until chilled. Fill four tall glasses with ice cubes. Pour ¼ cup of chai mix into each glass (or strain first if you prefer), then add 1 cup almond milk into each glass.

tip The chai mix can be stored in the fridge for up to 2 weeks.

FAT FIGHTER

SPICY BENEFITS

CHAMOMILE & LEMON ICED TEA

PREP + COOK TIME **25 MINUTES (+ REFRIGERATION)**

MAKES **1 LITRE (4 CUPS)**

Bring 1.25 litres (5 cups) of water to the boil in a medium saucepan; remove from heat. Add ⅓ cup dried chamomile flowers (or 3 tea bags), ¼ cup fresh lemon thyme sprigs and 4 slices lemon. Stir in 1 tablespoon raw honey until honey dissolves. Cover; steep for 20 minutes. Strain tea; refrigerate for at least 1 hour or until cooled. Serve tea mixture over ice with slices of lemon and extra sprigs fresh lemon thyme.

tip Chamomile tea is known for its soothing and calming effect, making this the perfect bedtime drink.

STRAWBERRY & BASIL ICED TEA

PREP + COOK TIME **10 MINUTES (+ REFRIGERATION)**

MAKES **1.25 LITRES (5 CUPS)**

Bring 1 litre (4 cups) water to the boil in a medium saucepan; remove from heat. Add 3 white tea bags and ½ cup fresh basil leaves; cover, steep for 5 minutes. Remove and discard basil and tea bags. Cool tea in the refrigerator. Blend 250g (8 ounces) ripe, hulled strawberries, ¼ cup of the cooled infused tea and 2 teaspoons stevia granules until smooth; strain through a fine sieve to remove seeds. Stir strawberry puree into remaining cooled tea with 2 tablespoons lemon juice. Half fill a large jug with ice, top with 2 sprigs fresh basil and 10 halved strawberries; stir in tea mixture.

tip White tea is one of the least processed of all teas; buds and leaves are allowed to dry naturally before being processed to produce a delicate taste.

SLEEP AID

TUMMY SOOTHER

GREEN TEA &
APPLE JUICE

PREP TIME **20 MINUTES (+ REFRIGERATION)** SERVES **2 (MAKES 2 CUPS)**

1 GREEN TEA BAG
¾ CUP (180ML) BOILING WATER
¾ CUP (180ML) CHILLED WATER
1 MEDIUM GREEN-SKINNED
   APPLE (150G), PEELED,
   HALVED, CORED
¼ TEASPOON FINELY GRATED
   FRESH GINGER
2 TABLESPOONS HONEY
2 TABLESPOONS FRESH
   MINT LEAVES
ICE-CUBES, TO SERVE

1 Place tea bag in a heatproof jug with the boiling water. Stand for 10 minutes to infuse. Remove and discard tea bag. Add the chilled water; refrigerate until cold.
2 Place iced tea in a high-powdered juice blender with apple, ginger, honey and mint; blend until smooth. Pour into glasses; top with ice-cubes.

nutritional count per serving
0.3g total fat (0g saturated fat); 510kJ (122 cal); 30g carbohydrate; 0.5g protein; 1.2g fibre

STRAWBERRY
SOY SHAKE

PREP + COOK TIME **10 MINUTES** SERVES **2**

125G (4 OUNCES) STRAWBERRIES
1½ CUPS (375ML) REDUCED-FAT
   SOY MILK
150G (4½ OUNCES) FIRM
   SILKEN TOFU
1 TABLESPOON HONEY

1 Blend 50g (1½ ounces) of the strawberries until smooth; reserve.
2 Place remaining strawberries in a blender with milk, tofu and honey; blend until smooth.
3 Pour into glasses; drizzle with reserved strawberry puree.

nutritional count per serving
2.9g total fat (0.4g saturated fat); 832kJ (199 cal); 29.7g carbohydrate; 14.1g protein; 3.5g fibre

tip Tofu is high in protein, low in fat and high in phytoestrogens.

GREEN
SUPER JUICE

PREP TIME **5 MINUTES** SERVES **3**

Blend 1 chopped lebanese cucumber (130g), 2 trimmed celery sticks (200g), 2 large trimmed kale leaves, 50g (1½oz) spinach leaves, 1 medium (150g) cored green apple, ½ peeled lemon, 1 sprig fresh mint, 1 cup coconut water and 1 cup ice-cubes on high speed for 1 minute or until smooth. If required, stop the blender and push the ingredients down before blending again.

tip Coconut water is available from most supermarkets, in the refrigerated section and alongside other long life milks.

ALMOND &
AVOCADO PROTEIN
SMOOTHIE

PREP TIME **5 MINUTES** SERVES **2**

Blend 1 cup unsweetened almond milk, 1 tablespoon vanilla-flavoured protein powder, 2 tablespoons almond butter, ½ medium ripe avocado, 1 tablespoon honey, ½ medium banana and 1 cup ice cubes on high speed for 1 minute or until smooth.

tip You can use your favourite nut milk or other milk, if you prefer.

FULL OF FOLATE

PROTEIN RICH

CREAMY RASPBERRY SMOOTHIE

PREP TIME **5 MINUTES (+ STANDING)** SERVES **2**

Place ⅔ cup (100g) raw cashews in a medium bowl; cover with cold water. Stand at room temperature for 3 hours. Drain; rinse well. Blend drained cashews with 1 cup coconut water, 1 cup frozen raspberries, 1 tablespoon maple syrup, ½ peeled lime and 1 cup ice-cubes for 1 minute or until smooth.

tip Coconut water is available from most supermarkets, in the refrigerated section and alongside other long life milks.

SUMMER SUNRISE

PREP TIME **10 MINUTES** SERVES **2**

In this order, place ½ cup coconut water and the juice of 1 medium orange, then 1 medium cored apple, ½ small peeled and cored ripe pineapple and 1cm (½-in) piece sliced fresh ginger in a blender. Add 1 cup ice-cubes; blend on high speed for 1 minute or until smooth.

tip Coconut water is available from most supermarkets, in the refrigerated section and alongside other long life milks.

IMMUNE BOOSTER

HEALTHY HEART

TROPICAL
FRUIT SMOOTHIE

PREP TIME **10 MINUTES** SERVES **2**

½ CUP (125ML) FRESH
  ORANGE JUICE
½ SMALL PINEAPPLE (450G),
  CHOPPED COARSELY
⅓ CUP (80ML) STRAINED
  PASSIONFRUIT JUICE (SEE TIP)
1 CUP (280G) LOW-FAT YOGHURT
1 TABLESPOON WHEAT GERM
CRUSHED ICE, TO SERVE

1 Blend ingredients until smooth.
2 Pour mixture into glasses filled
with crushed ice; top with extra
passionfruit, if you like.

nutritional count per serving
0.8g total fat (0.2g saturated fat);
769kJ (184 cal); 25.3g carbohydrate;
11.1g protein; 10.1g fibre

*tip To make the passionfruit
juice, scoop the pulp from
about 5 passionfruit into a
fine sieve over a small jug.
Press to extract as much juice
as possible; discard seeds.*

WEIGHT
CONTROL

CHERRY &
WALNUT
SMOOTHIE

PREP TIME **15 MINUTES (+ STANDING)** SERVES **4**

You need to start this recipe the day before.

½ CUP (50G) WALNUTS
⅓ CUP (55G) ALMOND KERNELS
1¾ CUPS (430ML) WATER
750G (1½ POUNDS) FROZEN PITTED CHERRIES
2 TEASPOONS PURE MAPLE SYRUP
1 TABLESPOON BLACK CHIA SEEDS
¼ CUP (25G) WALNUTS, EXTRA, CHOPPED COARSELY
CRUSHED ICE, TO SERVE

1 Rub walnuts in a clean tea towel to remove most of the skins. Place walnuts, almonds and the water in a medium bowl; cover, stand overnight.

2 Blend nut mixture for 2 minutes or until as smooth as possible. Strain mixture through a muslin or tea-towel-lined sieve over a medium jug, twist and press the cloth to extract as much nut milk as possible. Discard remaining solids.

3 Blend nut milk, cherries and syrup until smooth. Pour into 1-cup glasses; top with chia seeds, extra walnuts and crushed ice. Serve immediately, with fresh cherries, if you like.

nutritional count per serving
20.5g total fat (1.3g saturated fat); 1422kJ (339 cal); 25.7g carbohydrate; 7.7g protein; 1.2g fibre

tips For a thicker smoothie, blend the chia seeds with the other smoothie ingredients. You can make other nut milks using 105g (3½ ounces) total of your favourite nuts and seeds and 1¾ cups (430ml) water.

HORCHATA
PORRIDGE SHAKE

PREP + COOK TIME **15 MINUTES (+ REFRIGERATION)** SERVES **4 (MAKES 1 LITRE)**

You need to start this recipe the night before. This shake is perfect for a breakfast on the go – simply pour into a bottle, jar or jug with a lid and away you go.

1 VANILLA BEAN
1 LITRE (4 CUPS) UNSWEETENED ALMOND MILK
1 CUP (90G) ROLLED OATS
1 TABLESPOON RAW HONEY
½ TEASPOON SEA SALT
1 TABLESPOON ROLLED OATS, EXTRA
⅓ CUP (24G) FLAKED ALMONDS
½ TEASPOON GROUND CINNAMON

1 Split vanilla beans in half lengthways; using the tip of a small knife, scrape out seeds. Combine vanilla seeds and pod with almond milk, oats and honey in a medium jug. Cover; refrigerate overnight.

2 Preheat oven to 180°C/350°F. Place extra oats on an oven tray; roast for 5 minutes. Add almonds; roast for another 5 minutes or until lightly golden.

3 Discard vanilla bean from milk mixture. Blend or process milk mixture until smooth; stir in salt.

4 Pour shake into four glasses, top with roasted almond mixture; sprinkle with cinnamon. Serve immediately.

nutritional count per serving
8.7g total fat (0.6g saturated fat); 829kJ (198 cal); 27g carbohydrate; 8.6g protein; 3.5g fibre

tip For a quick version, skip the oats (and the overnight refrigeration); blend chilled milk, vanilla seeds, honey and salt until well combined. Serve immediately.

POWER STARTS

FRIED EGGS & SPICED
YOGHURT SAUCE

PREP + COOK TIME **15 MINUTES** SERVES **2**

2 TABLESPOONS OLIVE OIL
1 CLOVE GARLIC, CRUSHED
½ TEASPOON DRIED MINT
½ TEASPOON SWEET PAPRIKA
1 TEASPOON CUMIN SEEDS
COOKING-OIL SPRAY
4 FREE-RANGE EGGS
½ CUP (140G) GREEK-STYLE
**   YOGHURT, WARMED (SEE TIPS)**
1 TABLESPOON DUKKAH
2 TABLESPOONS LOOSELY
**   PACKED FRESH MINT LEAVES**
2 WHOLEMEAL PITTA BREADS
**   (170G), CHAR-GRILLED**
**   (SEE TIPS)**

1 Heat oil in a 22cm (9-inch) frying pan (base measurement) over medium heat; cook garlic, dried mint and spices, stirring for 1 minute or until fragrant. Transfer spiced oil to a small bowl.

2 Wipe out pan with paper towel. Lightly spray pan with cooking oil. Heat pan over medium heat; cook eggs for 4 minutes or until whites are set and yolks remain runny. Add yoghurt to pan; remove from heat.

3 Sprinkle eggs with dukkah and fresh mint; drizzle with spiced oil. Season. Serve with pitta bread.

nutritional count per serving
38.6g total fat (9.6g saturated fat); 2802kJ (670 cal); 51.6g carbohydrate; 25.7g protein; 7g fibre

tips Place the yoghurt in a covered microwave-safe bowl; warm in the microwave oven for 20-30 seconds. Char-grill the pitta bread, on both sides, in a heated grill pan or on a barbecue grill plate.

RED FRUIT SALAD
WITH CHAI YOGHURT

PREP + COOK TIME **15 MINUTES (+ COOLING & REFRIGERATION)** SERVES **4**

½ CUP (125ML) WATER

2 TABLESPOONS HONEY

1 CINNAMON STICK

3CM (1¼-INCH) PIECE FRESH
   GINGER, CUT INTO THIN
   MATCHSTICKS

2 CARDAMOM PODS, BRUISED

2 WHOLE CLOVES

1 WHOLE STAR ANISE

500G (1 POUND) WATERMELON,
   RIND REMOVED, CUT INTO
   SMALL WEDGES

250G (8 OUNCES) STRAWBERRIES,
   HALVED

250G (8 OUNCES) RED SEEDLESS
   GRAPES, HALVED

250G (8 OUNCES) CHERRIES,
   HALVED, SEEDS REMOVED

1½ CUPS (420G) GREEK-STYLE
   YOGHURT

¼ CUP (30G) SLIVERED
   PISTACHIOS

MICRO HERBS, TO SERVE
   (OPTIONAL)

1 Stir the water, honey, cinnamon, ginger, cardamom, cloves and star anise in a small saucepan over medium heat until honey dissolves. Bring to the boil. Reduce heat; simmer, uncovered, for 2 minutes or until chai syrup reduces by half. Remove from heat; cool completely.

2 Place watermelon, strawberries, grapes and cherries in a bowl with half the cooled chai syrup; toss to combine. Refrigerate for 10 minutes.

3 Swirl remaining chai syrup through yoghurt in a small bowl.

4 Serve fruit salad topped with pistachios and micro herbs, along with the chai yogurt.

nutritional count per serving
10.5g total fat (4.5g saturated fat); 1450kJ (346 cal); 51.3g carbohydrate; 9.2g protein; 4.8g fibre

tips Remove the whole spices from the chai syrup before use if you prefer. Micro herbs are avialable from most major supermarkets and greengrocers.

FRENCH TOAST
WITH POACHED CHERRIES

PREP + COOK TIME **30 MINUTES** SERVES **4**

4 FREE-RANGE EGGS
⅓ CUP (80ML) MILK
1½ TABLESPOONS COCONUT OIL
8 X 2.5CM (1-INCH) THICK SLICES
WHOLEGRAIN BREAD (300G)
⅓ CUP (95G) GREEK-STYLE
YOGHURT
POACHED CHERRIES
1 VANILLA BEAN
2 MEDIUM ORANGES (480G)
½ CUP (125ML) WATER
¼ CUP (60ML) PURE MAPLE
SYRUP
300G (9½ OUNCES) CHERRIES

1 Make poached cherries.
2 Meanwhile, preheat oven to 120°C/250°F. Place a large wire rack over an oven tray.
3 Lightly whisk eggs and reserved vanilla seeds (from poached cherries) in a medium bowl until combined; whisk in milk.
4 Heat half the coconut oil in a large frying pan over medium heat until melted. Dip four bread slices, one at a time, into egg mixture, turning until soaked; drain away excess. Cook bread in pan for 2 minutes each side or until browned and firm to touch in the centre. Transfer to warm wire rack; keep warm in oven.
5 Repeat step 4 with remaining oil, bread and egg mixture.
6 Serve french toast with poached cherries and yoghurt.

poached cherries Split vanilla bean lengthways; scrape out seeds. Reserve seeds for french toast. Thinly peel a strip of rind from one orange. Squeeze juice from oranges; you will need ½ cup juice. Place vanilla bean, rind, juice, the water and syrup in a small saucepan; bring to a simmer. Add cherries; simmer, uncovered, for 3 minutes. Remove from heat; stand for 10 minutes.

nutritional count per serving
17.8g total fat (10g saturated fat); 1953kJ (470 cal); 57.5g carbohydrate; 16.3g protein; 6.4g fibre

tips Use any type of milk you prefer – almond, rice, soy, goat's and cow's milk are all suitable. You can use olive oil instead of the coconut oil.

SPICED COUSCOUS WITH
PASSIONFRUIT
YOGHURT

PREP + COOK TIME **25 MINUTES** SERVES **4**

- **1 CUP (200G) WHOLEMEAL COUSCOUS**
- **2 TEASPOONS EXTRA VIRGIN OLIVE OIL**
- **1 TEASPOON MIXED SPICE**
- **¼ TEASPOON ALLSPICE**
- **¼ CUP (90G) HONEY**
- **1 CUP (250ML) BOILING WATER**
- **½ CUP (50G) WALNUTS, TOASTED**
- **¾ CUP (200G) GREEK-STYLE YOGHURT**
- **2 TABLESPOONS PASSIONFRUIT PULP**
- **2 MEDIUM ORANGES (480G), PEELED, SLICED THINLY**
- **⅓ CUP (50G) BLUEBERRIES**
- **¼ CUP FRESH MINT LEAVES**

1 Combine couscous, oil, mixed spice, allspice, a pinch of salt, honey and the boiling water in a medium heatproof bowl; stand for 5 minutes or until liquid is absorbed, fluffing with a fork occasionally.

2 Cover couscous with plastic wrap. Microwave on HIGH (100%) for 30 seconds; fluff couscous with a fork to separate grains. Repeat process two or three times or until couscous is very fluffy. Stir in walnuts.

3 Meanwhile, combine yoghurt and passionfruit in a small bowl.

4 Serve couscous topped with orange slices, blueberries, yoghurt mixture and mint.

nutritional count per serving
14.6g total fat (2.8g saturated fat); 1993kJ (476 cal); 73.7g carbohydrate; 11g protein; 4.4g fibre

tip Microwaving the couscous after it has absorbed the water produces a lovely light couscous

THIS **BREAKFAST SORBET** INCLUDES A SERVING OF VEGETABLES, GIVING YOU A BOOST OF PHYTONUTRIENTS FROM THE RICH RED OF BEETROOT.

CHIA BIRCHER WITH
GRANOLA &
POMEGRANATE

PREP + COOK TIME **25 MINUTES (+ REFRIGERATION)** SERVES **4**

You will need to start this recipe the day before.

160G (5 OUNCES) RASPBERRIES
2 CUPS (560G) LOW-FAT GREEK-STYLE YOGHURT
¼ CUP (40G) WHITE CHIA SEEDS
½ TEASPOON VANILLA EXTRACT
1 TABLESPOON PURE MAPLE SYRUP
¾ CUP (60G) TRADITIONAL ROLLED OATS
½ CUP (40G) SLICED RAW ALMONDS
¼ TEASPOON GROUND CINNAMON
1 MEDIUM POMEGRANATE (320G), SEEDS REMOVED (SEE TIPS)

1 Reserve 12 of the raspberries. Mash remaining raspberries in a medium bowl with yoghurt until combined. Stir in chia seeds, extract and 2 teaspoons of the maple syrup. Cover; refrigerate overnight.
2 Preheat oven to 200°C/400°F.
3 Place oats on an oven tray; bake for 5 minutes or until lightly browned. Add almonds, cinnamon and remaining maple syrup; mix well. Bake for another 5 minutes or until nuts are golden. Cool.
4 Spoon half the chia yoghurt mixture into four 1 cup (250ml) jars. Top with half the pomegranate seeds and half the granola. Repeat layering with remaining chia yoghurt mixture, pomegranate seeds and granola. Serve topped with reserved raspberries.

nutritional count per serving
18.7g total fat (5.8g saturated fat); 1849kJ (442 cal); 48g carbohydrate; 13.5g protein; 11.5g fibre

tips To remove pomegranate seeds, cut pomegranate in half crossways; hold it, cut-side down, in the palm of your hand over a bowl, then hit the outside firmly with a wooden spoon. The seeds should fall out easily; discard any white pith that falls out with them. Make a double batch of the granola and store in an airtight container for up to 1 week.

RICOTTA PANCAKES
WITH TOMATO & ROCKET

PREP + COOK TIME **45 MINUTES** SERVES **4**

300G (9½ OUNCES) BABY TRUSS ROMA (EGG) TOMATOES
2 TABLESPOONS EXTRA VIRGIN OLIVE OIL
1 CUP (240G) RICOTTA
1 EGG
1¼ CUPS (310ML) MILK
1¼ CUPS (185G) SELF-RAISING FLOUR
½ CUP COARSELY CHOPPED FRESH BASIL
¼ CUP (20G) GRATED PARMESAN
30G (1 OUNCE) BUTTER
1 TABLESPOON WHITE BALSAMIC VINEGAR
250G (8 OUNCES) ROCKET (ARUGULA)
½ SMALL RED ONION (50G), SLICED THINLY

1 Preheat oven to 220°C/425°F.

2 Place tomatoes in a small baking dish; drizzle with half the oil, then season. Roast for 10 minutes or until skins just split.

3 Whisk ricotta and egg in a medium bowl until combined. Whisk in milk, then flour. Stir in basil and parmesan; season.

4 Melt a little of the butter in a large frying pan over medium heat. Pour ¼-cups of mixture into pan, allowing room for spreading. Cook pancakes for 2 minutes each side or until golden and cooked through. Stack pancakes; cover to keep warm.

5 Wipe out pan with paper towel. Repeat step 4 with the remaining butter and batter to make a total of 12 pancakes.

6 Place rocket and onion in a medium bowl with vinegar and remaining oil, season to taste; toss gently to combine.

7 Serve warm pancakes topped with rocket mixture, tomatoes and any remaining dressing.

nutritional count per serving
21.7g total fat (11g saturated fat); 1920kJ (459 cal); 44.5g carbohydrate; 19.2g protein; 4.1g fibre

tip Wipe the pan clean with paper towel between each batch of pancakes so they don't over-brown.

MIXED MUSHROOMS
WITH SMOKED SALMON

PREP + COOK TIME **20 MINUTES** SERVES **4**

- 20G (¾ OUNCE) SUNFLOWER SEEDS, CHOPPED
- 20G (¾ OUNCE) PEPITAS (PUMPKIN SEEDS), CHOPPED
- 2½ TABLESPOONS OLIVE OIL
- 600G (1¼ POUNDS) SWISS BROWN MUSHROOMS, SLICED THICKLY
- 600G (1¼ POUNDS) OYSTER MUSHROOMS
- 1 LARGE CLOVE GARLIC, CRUSHED
- 1 FRESH LONG RED CHILLI, SEEDED, CHOPPED FINELY
- 1 TABLESPOON WATER
- 2 TEASPOONS LEMON JUICE
- 4 FREE-RANGE EGGS
- 1 TABLESPOON VINEGAR
- 200G (6½ OUNCES) SMOKED SALMON
- 2 TABLESPOONS FRESH CHERVIL LEAVES

1 Heat a large frying pan over medium heat. Add sunflower seeds and pepitas; cook, stirring, for 2 minutes or until seeds are toasted. Remove from pan.

2 Heat 1 tablespoon of the oil in same pan over high heat, add half the mushrooms; cook, stirring occasionally, for 4 minutes or until browned lightly. Transfer to a large bowl; cover with foil to keep warm. Repeat with another tablespoon of the oil and remaining mushrooms.

3 Return all mushrooms to pan, stir in garlic, chilli and the water; cook for 1 minute or until fragrant. Remove pan from heat; stir in lemon juice; season. Transfer mixture to bowl; cover with foil to keep warm.

4 Meanwhile, to poach eggs, half-fill a large, deep frying pan with water, add vinegar; bring to a gentle simmer. Break 1 egg into a cup. Using a wooden spoon, make a whirlpool in the water; slide egg into whirlpool. Repeat with a second egg. Cook eggs for 3 minutes or until whites are set and the yolks remain runny. Remove eggs with a slotted spoon; drain on a paper-towel-lined plate. Keep warm. Repeat poaching with remaining eggs.

5 Spoon mushroom mixture among serving plates; top with smoked salmon, toasted seed mixture, eggs and chervil. Season.

nutritional count per serving
24.3g total fat (4.4g saturated fat); 1596kJ (381 cal); 4.7g carbohydrate; 30.7g protein; 11.6g fibre

HUEVOS RANCHEROS

PREP + COOK TIME **45 MINUTES** SERVES **4**

1 TABLESPOON EXTRA VIRGIN
   OLIVE OIL
1 MEDIUM ONION (150G),
   CHOPPED
250G (8 OUNCES) MINI RED
   CAPSICUMS (BELL PEPPERS),
   QUARTERED
2 CLOVES GARLIC, CRUSHED
2 TEASPOONS GROUND CUMIN
1KG (2 POUNDS) RIPE VINE-
   RIPENED TOMATOES,
   CHOPPED COARSELY
400G (12½ OUNCES) CANNED
   RED KIDNEY BEANS,
   DRAINED, RINSED
2 TABLESPOONS COARSELY
   CHOPPED FRESH CORIANDER
   (CILANTRO) LEAVES
100G (3 OUNCES) DRAINED
   PERSIAN FETTA, CRUMBLED
4 FREE-RANGE EGGS
1 FRESH GREEN JALAPEÑO
   CHILLI, SLICED THINLY
⅓ CUP LOOSELY PACKED FRESH
   CORIANDER (CILANTRO)
   SPRIGS, EXTRA

1 Heat oil in a large frying pan over medium heat; cook onion and capsicum, stirring, for 5 minutes or until soft. Add garlic and cumin; cook, stirring, until fragrant. Stir in tomatoes and beans; simmer, uncovered, for 20 minutes or until sauce thickens. Season to taste. Stir in coriander.

2 Meanwhile, preheat oven to 180°C/350°F; place a 1 litre (4-cup) ovenproof dish in the oven while preheating.

3 Pour hot tomato mixture into hot dish, top with fetta; make four indents in the mixture. Break eggs into a cup, one at a time, sliding each into an indent. Top with chilli.

4 Bake for 8 minutes or until whites of the eggs are set and the yolks are just beginning to set. (The cooking time will vary depending on what your ovenproof dish is made from, and may take up to 15 minutes to cook.) Serve huevos rancheros topped with extra coriander.

nutritional count per serving
16.7g total fat (6.2g saturated fat); 1356kJ (324 cal); 19.3g carbohydrate; 19.6g protein; 9.5g fibre

tips The tomato mixture can be made a day ahead; reheat before adding the eggs. If you can't find mini capsicums, use 1 medium-sized capsicum instead and cut into chunky pieces.

serving suggestion Serve with wholegrain tortillas.

BANANA
BREAKFAST
SORBET

PREP + COOK TIME **15 MINUTES (+ FREEZING)** SERVES **4**

**4 MEDIUM FROZEN BANANAS
(800G), BROKEN INTO PIECES**

**500G (1 POUND) FROZEN
STRAWBERRIES**

**1 SMALL BEETROOT (BEETS)
(100G), PEELED, CHOPPED**

**1 TABLESPOON FINELY GRATED
FRESH GINGER**

**2 CUPS (500ML) UNSWEETENED
ALMOND MILK**

**250G (8 OUNCES) FRESH
STRAWBERRIES, HALVED**

**2 MEDIUM GOLDEN KIWIFRUITS
(170G), PEELED, SLICED**

**1 TABLESPOON WHITE
CHIA SEEDS**

1 Working in two batches, place bananas, frozen strawberries, beetroot, ginger and almond milk in a blender; blend until smooth.

2 Pour mixture into a freezerproof container; cover with plastic wrap. Freeze for 6 hours or overnight until firm.

3 Working in two batches, scoop sorbet into blender; blend until smooth.

4 Pour sorbet into bowls; top with fresh strawberries, kiwifruit and chia seeds. Serve immediately.

nutritional count per serving
15.8g total fat (1g saturated fat);
1466kJ (350 cal); 36.4g carbohydrate;
10.8g protein; 10.5g fibre

tips Keep chopped bananas in a resealable plastic bag in the freezer to make early morning blending faster and easier. You can replace almond milk with any milk you prefer. Serve the sorbet topped with any of your favourite fruit. Sorbet can be stored in the freezer for up to 1 week.

MANDARIN & CARDAMOM
NO-GRAIN GRANOLA

PREP + COOK TIME **30 MINUTES (+ COOLING)** SERVES **4 (MAKES 5 CUPS)**

2 MEDIUM MANDARINS (400G)
½ CUP (80G) ALMOND KERNELS, CHOPPED COARSELY
½ CUP (80G) SHELLED PISTACHIOS, CHOPPED
½ CUP (60G) PECANS, CHOPPED COARSELY
¼ CUP (50G) PEPITAS (PUMPKIN SEEDS)
½ CUP (60G) GROUND ALMONDS
1 TABLESPOON GROUND CARDAMOM
½ CUP (120G) COCONUT OIL, MELTED
2 TABLESPOONS HONEY
½ TEASPOON SEA SALT
2½ CUPS (125G) COCONUT FLAKES

1 Preheat oven to 160°C/325°F. Grease and line two large oven trays with baking paper.

2 Peel rind from mandarins. Using a small sharp knife, remove the white pith. Cut rind into thick strips. Combine mandarin rind with remaining ingredients except the coconut flakes in a large bowl. Using your hands, squeeze and rub the mixture together to release the oil from the mandarin rind; fold in coconut flakes. Spread mixture evenly between trays.

3 Bake muesli for 20 minutes, stirring occasionally into clumps, or until lightly golden. Cool on trays for 15 minutes to crisp slightly.

4 Serve muesli with milk or yoghurt and fresh fruit such as mandarin and blood orange.

nutritional count per serving
84.5g total fat (39g saturated fat); 4052kJ (968 cal); 32g carbohydrate; 16.9g protein; 8.5g fibre

tips Muesli can be stored in an airtight container for up to 10 days. Divide muesli into individual resealable plastic bags for a handy snack. Use orange rind instead of mandarin, if you like.

BEING HEALTHY
AND ACTIVE
ISN'T A FAD
OR A TREND,
IT'S A LIFESTYLE.

THREE-GRAIN
MAPLE SYRUP
PORRIDGE

PREP + COOK TIME **50 MINUTES** SERVES **4**

1 CUP (160G) BROWN RICE
½ CUP (100G) PEARL BARLEY
½ CUP (45G) STEEL CUT OATS
1.25 LITRES (5 CUPS) WATER
1 CINNAMON STICK, HALVED
½ VANILLA BEAN, SEEDS
SCRAPED
½ TEASPOON SALT
½ CUP (125ML) MILK
2 TABLESPOONS PURE MAPLE
SYRUP
1 RIPE PERSIMMON (120G),
SLICED THINLY
125G (4 OUNCES) BLUEBERRIES
¼ CUP (60G) POMEGRANATE
SEEDS (SEE TIPS)
¼ CUP (35G) HAZELNUTS,
ROASTED, CHOPPED
¾ CUP (200G) VANILLA
YOGHURT
2 TABLESPOONS PURE MAPLE
SYRUP, EXTRA
PINCH OF GROUND CINNAMON

1 Combine rice, barley, oats, the water, cinnamon stick, vanilla bean and seeds and salt in a medium saucepan over high heat; bring to the boil. Reduce heat to low; simmer, covered, for 40 minutes, stirring occasionally to prevent sticking to base of pan, or until grains are tender with a slight bite.

2 Stir in milk and maple syrup; cook, stirring for 5 minutes or until heated through.

3 Serve porridge topped with persimmon slices, blueberries, pomegranate seeds, hazelnuts and yoghurt; drizzle with extra maple syrup and sprinkle with ground cinnamon.

nutritional count per serving
10.9g total fat (2.5g saturated fat); 2136kJ (510 cal); 87g carbohydrate; 11.8g protein; 8.4g fibre

tips To remove the seeds from a pomegranate, cut a pomegranate in half crossways; hold it, cut-side down, in the palm of your hand over a bowl, then hit the outside firmly with a wooden spoon. The seeds should fall out easily; discard any white pith that falls out with them. Pomegranate seeds will keep in the fridge for up to a week. Cool any leftover porridge and keep, covered, in the fridge for up to 3 days. Stir in a little extra milk just before serving.

APPLE PIE PANCAKES WITH
BLACKBERRY COMPOTE

PREP + COOK TIME **35 MINUTES (+ COOLING)** SERVES **4**

1 CUP (135G) FROZEN BLACKBERRIES
⅓ CUP (80ML) PURE MAPLE SYRUP
1 CUP (150G) WHOLEMEAL SPELT FLOUR
2 TEASPOONS BAKING POWDER
1 TEASPOON GROUND CINNAMON
½ TEASPOON MIXED SPICE
1 CUP (250ML) BUTTERMILK
1 FREE-RANGE EGG, BEATEN LIGHTLY
2 TEASPOONS VANILLA EXTRACT
1 MEDIUM PINK LADY APPLE (150G), UNPEELED, GRATED
MICRO MINT, TO SERVE

1 Combine blackberries and half the maple syrup in a small saucepan; bring to the boil. Reduce heat; simmer, stirring occasionally, for 10 minutes or until berries soften. Remove from heat; cool.

2 Sift flour, baking powder, spices and a pinch of salt into a medium bowl; gradually whisk in combined buttermilk, egg, extract and remaining maple syrup until batter is smooth. Fold in apple.

3 Heat an oiled, medium non-stick frying pan over medium heat. Pour ¼-cup of batter for each pancake into pan; cook until bubbles appear on the surface. Turn; cook until browned lightly. Remove from pan; cover to keep warm. Repeat with remaining batter to make a total of eight pancakes.

4 Serve pancakes with blackberry compote and mint.

nutritional count per serving
3.5g total fat (1.4g saturated fat); 1271kJ (303 cal); 50.5g carbohydrate; 10.3g protein; 6.7g fibre

tip You could use frozen mixed berries instead of blackberries.

GLUTEN-FREE
HAM & GREEN
ONION FRITTERS

PREP + COOK TIME **20 MINUTES** SERVES **4**

For a vegetarian option, use frozen peas or corn instead of the ham.

250G (8 OUNCES) RED GRAPE TOMATOES
1 TEASPOON BALSAMIC VINEGAR
1½ TABLESPOONS OLIVE OIL
1 CUP (135G) GLUTEN-FREE SELF-RAISING FLOUR
¾ CUP (180ML) SOY MILK
250G (8 OUNCES) GLUTEN-FREE SHAVED HAM, CHOPPED FINELY
4 GREEN ONIONS (SCALLIONS), SLICED THINLY
1 LARGE AVOCADO (320G), CHOPPED COARSELY

1 Preheat oven to 200°C/400°F.
2 Place tomatoes on an oven tray; drizzle with vinegar and 1 teaspoon of the oil. Season. Roast for 15 minutes or until tomatoes just soften.
3 Sift flour into a large bowl. Gradually add milk, in batches, stirring after each addition. Add ham and green onion; stir to combine. Season.
4 Heat remaining oil in a large non-stick frying pan over medium heat. Spoon ¼-cups of batter into pan; cook for 2½ minutes each side or until golden brown and cooked through. Repeat with remaining batter to make a total of eight fritters.
5 Serve fritters with avocado and roasted tomatoes.

nutritional count per serving
24.8g total fat (5.6g saturated fat); 1822kJ (435 cal); 31.5g carbohydrate; 20.1g protein

tips You can make these fritters with regular self-raising flour if you don't need to make them gluten free, though you may need to use less milk. Use any type of milk you prefer.

BANANA & CHOCOLATE
ALMOND TOASTIE

PREP + COOK TIME **15 MINUTES** MAKES **2**

4 SQUARE SLICES SOURDOUGH BREAD (180G) (SEE TIPS)
10G (½ OUNCE) BUTTER, SOFTENED
2 TABLESPOONS ALMOND BUTTER
1 TEASPOON CACAO POWDER
2 TEASPOONS RICE MALT SYRUP
1 MEDIUM BANANA (180G), SLICED THINLY
¼ TEASPOON GROUND CINNAMON

1 Preheat a jaffle or sandwich maker.
2 Spread one side of each bread slice with butter.
3 Stir almond butter, cacao and syrup in a small bowl until smooth.
4 Place two slices of bread buttered-side-down on a board; spread half the almond butter mixture on each slice, then top with banana, leaving a 1cm (½-inch) border. Top with remaining bread slices, buttered-side-up.
5 Cook sandwiches in jaffle maker for 5 minutes or until golden. Serve cut in half, dusted with cinnamon.

nutritional count per toastie
16.4g total fat (4.2g saturated fat); 2082kJ (498 cal); 69.6g carbohydrate; 16.3g protein; 4.6g fibre

tips Use any bread you prefer – wholemeal, wholegrain and rye would all taste great, just make sure the slices are square to fit the jaffle maker. Use any nut butter you prefer instead of the almond butter. Other great alternatives are coconut butter or ricotta, especially if you have a nut allergy.

GLUTEN-FREE
BREAKFAST
WRAPS

PREP + COOK TIME **50 MINUTES** MAKES **4**

You will need a sandwich press with two flat elements.

COOKING-OIL SPRAY
4 FREE-RANGE EGGS
4 RINDLESS BACON SLICES (260G)
1 TABLESPOON DAIRY-FREE SPREAD
150G (4½ OUNCES) BUTTON MUSHROOMS, SLICED THINLY
60G (2 OUNCES) BABY SPINACH LEAVES
2 TABLESPOONS GLUTEN-FREE BARBECUE SAUCE
GLUTEN-FREE WRAPS
2 EGGS
1 CUP (135G) GLUTEN-FREE SELF-RAISING FLOUR
⅓ CUP (50G) BUCKWHEAT FLOUR
⅓ CUP (45G) GLUTEN-FREE PLAIN (ALL-PURPOSE) FLOUR
⅓ CUP (50G) 100% CORN (MAIZE) CORNFLOUR (CORNSTARCH)
1½ TEASPOONS SALT
⅔ CUP (160ML) SOY MILK
⅔ CUP (160ML) WATER

1 Make gluten-free wraps.
2 Spray a medium frying pan with oil; cook eggs over medium heat. Transfer to a plate; cover to keep warm.
3 Cook bacon in the same pan until crisp; transfer to the plate, cover to keep warm. Melt dairy-free spread in same heated pan; cook mushrooms over medium heat for 5 minutes or until just softened.
4 Divide spinach, mushrooms and bacon between wraps; drizzle with barbecue sauce then top with egg. Season. Roll wraps to serve.

gluten-free wraps Beat eggs in a small bowl with an electric mixer until thick and pale. Stir in the sifted dry ingredients, and the combined milk and water, alternately, stirring until just combined; do not over mix. Heat a flat sandwich press until light indicates it is ready to use; spray with oil. Pour ⅓ cup of mixture in a circle shape onto press; fully close lid and cook for 2 minutes or until golden brown. Transfer to a plate. Repeat to make a total of four wraps.

nutritional count per wrap
20.6g total fat (6.5g saturated fat); 2148kJ (513 cal); 66.6g carbohydrate; 26.1g protein; 1.4g fibre

tips If you don't have a sandwich press, spread ⅓ cup of batter into a circle shape in a heated large frying pan; cook both sides until brown and cooked through. Unfilled wraps can be made a day ahead; store in the fridge in an airtight container, or freeze for up to 3 months. Reheat wraps in a heated frying pan until warmed through.

GLUTEN-FREE RASPBERRY
& BANANA BREAD

PREP + COOK TIME **1 HOUR 45 MINUTES (+ COOLING)** SERVES **8**

You need 3 large overripe bananas (690g) for the mashed banana in this recipe.

- **1½ CUPS (350G) MASHED BANANA**
- **½ CUP (125ML) VEGETABLE OIL**
- **½ CUP (125ML) SOY MILK**
- **2½ CUPS (335G) GLUTEN-FREE SELF-RAISING FLOUR**
- **1¼ CUPS (275G) FIRMLY PACKED BROWN SUGAR**
- **½ TEASPOON BICARBONATE OF SODA (BAKING SODA)**
- **1 CUP (80G) DESICCATED COCONUT**
- **1 CUP (150G) FROZEN RASPBERRIES**
- **20G (¾ OUNCE) DAIRY-FREE SPREAD**
- **1 LARGE BANANA (230G), SLICED THICKLY ON THE DIAGONAL**
- **⅓ CUP (100G) GOLDEN SYRUP**

1 Preheat oven to 180°C/375°F. Grease a 10cm x 20cm (4-inch x 8-inch) loaf pan; line base and long sides with baking paper, extending the paper 5cm (2 inches) over sides.

2 Combine mashed banana, oil and milk in a small bowl.

3 Combine sifted flour, sugar and bicarbonate of soda with coconut in a large bowl. Make a well in the centre. Pour banana mixture into well; stir to combine. Fold in raspberries until just combined. Spoon mixture into pan; smooth the surface.

4 Bake bread for 1¼ hours or until a skewer inserted into the centre comes out clean. Leave in pan for 5 minutes before turning, top-side up, onto a wire rack to cool.

5 Melt dairy-free spread in a large frying pan over high heat, add sliced banana; cook 1 minute each side or until caramelised. Thickly slice bread, top with banana; drizzle with golden syrup.

nutritional count per serving
23g total fat (7.4g saturated fat); 2464kJ (588 cal); 93.4g carbohydrate; 2.7g protein; 4.3g fibre

tips You can use your favourite dairy-free milk or other milk, if you prefer, and butter instead of the dairy-free spread. You can replace the raspberries with blueberries or chopped pear, or leave it out altogether. Cut the bread into portion-sized pieces and freeze in an airtight container for up to 3 months.

GREEN QUINOA
WITH SESAME EGGS

PREP + COOK TIME **25 MINUTES** SERVES **2**

- **½ CUP (100G) WHITE QUINOA, RINSED**
- **1 CUP (250G) CHICKEN OR VEGETABLE STOCK**
- **4 FREE-RANGE EGGS, AT ROOM TEMPERATURE**
- **2 TEASPOONS COCONUT OIL**
- **1 SMALL CLOVE GARLIC, CRUSHED**
- **1 FRESH SMALL RED CHILLI, CHOPPED FINELY**
- **2 CUPS (80G) THINLY SLICED KALE (SEE TIP)**
- **2 CUPS (90G) FIRMLY PACKED THINLY SLICED SILVER BEET (SWISS CHARD) (SEE TIP)**
- **1 TABLESPOON LEMON JUICE**
- **¼ CUP FINELY CHOPPED FRESH FLAT-LEAF PARSLEY**
- **1 TABLESPOON WHITE SESAME SEEDS**
- **1 TABLESPOON BLACK SESAME SEEDS**
- **1 TEASPOON SEA SALT FLAKES**

1 Place quinoa and stock in a medium saucepan; bring to the boil. Reduce heat to low-medium; simmer gently for 15 minutes or until most of the stock is absorbed. Remove from heat; cover, stand 5 minutes.

2 Meanwhile, cook eggs in a small saucepan of boiling water for 5 minutes. Remove immediately from pan; cool under cold running water for 30 seconds. Peel.

3 Heat coconut oil in a medium saucepan over medium heat, add garlic and chilli; cook stirring, for 2 minutes or until fragrant. Add kale and silver beet; stir until wilted. Stir in quinoa and juice; season to taste.

4 Combine parsley, sesame seeds and salt in a small bowl. Roll peeled eggs in parsley mixture.

5 Serve quinoa topped with eggs.

nutritional count per serving
23.8g total fat (8.6g saturated fat); 1957kJ (467cal); 35g carbohydrate; 25g protein; 7.6g fibre

tip You will need half a bunch of kale and half a bunch of silver beet for this recipe. Wash them both well before use.

5 WAYS WITH
COCONUT OIL

HAIR CARE
FOR DRY HAIR

Massage a few drops of coconut oil into your scalp to moisturise the skin, keeping dandruff at bay and your hair nice and shiny. For dry ends, rub a little coconut oil into them with your fingers for a deep leave-in conditioner.

Makeup Remover

THIS NATURAL CLEANSER IS IDEAL FOR ALL SKIN TYPES. STIR 2 TABLESPOONS COCONUT OIL, 2 TEASPOONS HONEY, 1 TEASPOON BICARBONATE OF SODA AND VANILLA ESSENTIAL OIL UNTIL SMOOTH. APPLY A SMALL AMOUNT TO YOUR FACE AND NECK, THEN LEAVE FOR 2 OR 3 MINUTES. WIPE OFF WITH A CLOTH AND WARM WATER.

BODY BUTTER COMBINE COCONUT OIL, HONEY AND GRATED ORANGE RIND UNTIL CREAMY. FOR A WHIPPED BODY BUTTER, MIX IN A BLENDER UNTIL FLUFFY. IT ALSO DOUBLES AS A SHAVING CREAM.

LIP BALM

Melt 2 tablespoons coconut oil, 2 tablespoons beeswax and 1 tablespoon shea butter over low heat. Stir in your favourite essential oil. Pour into lip balm jars and leave until set.

Hand & Nail Care
Rub a little coconut oil into your cuticles to soften before pushing them back, which helps your nails to grow. Use a little more oil to moisturise your hands.

BREAKFAST SALAD
WITH EGGS & KALE PESTO

PREP + COOK TIME **25 MINUTES** SERVES **2**

¾ CUP (45G) FIRMLY PACKED
  BABY LEAVES (SEE TIPS)
100G (3 OUNCES) BRUSSELS
  SPROUTS, SHAVED THINLY
1 CUP (150G) CRUNCHY COMBO
  SPROUT MIX
1 SMALL CARROT (80G),
  CUT INTO MATCHSTICKS
2 TABLESPOONS TOASTED
  SUNFLOWER SEEDS
2 TABLESPOONS APPLE
  CIDER VINEGAR
1½ TABLESPOONS AVOCADO OIL
1 TEASPOON RAW HONEY
1 TABLESPOON WHITE VINEGAR
4 FREE-RANGE EGGS
½ MEDIUM AVOCADO (125G),
  SLICED THINLY
KALE PESTO
⅓ CUP (55G) DRY-ROASTED
  ALMONDS
⅓ CUP (50G) ROASTED CASHEWS
2 SMALL CLOVES GARLIC
2 CUPS (80G) BABY KALE,
  CHOPPED COARSELY
½ CUP (125ML) EXTRA VIRGIN
  OLIVE OIL
1½ TABLESPOONS APPLE
  CIDER VINEGAR
¼ CUP (20G) FINELY GRATED
  PARMESAN

1 Make kale pesto.
2 Place baby leaves, brussels sprouts, sprout mix, carrot and seeds in a medium bowl; toss to combine. Whisk cider vinegar, 1 tablespoon of the oil and honey in a small bowl; season to taste. Add dressing to salad; toss to combine.
3 To poach eggs, half-fill a large, deep-frying pan with water, add white vinegar; bring to a gentle simmer. Break 1 egg into a cup. Using a wooden spoon, make a whirlpool in the water; slide egg into whirlpool. Repeat with remaining eggs. Cook eggs for 3 minutes or until whites are set and the yolks are runny. Remove eggs with a slotted spoon; drain on a paper-towel-lined plate.
4 Divide salad between serving bowls; top with eggs and avocado. Spoon pesto on eggs; drizzle with remaining oil.

kale pesto Pulse nuts and garlic in a food processor until coarsely chopped. Add kale, oil and vinegar; pulse to a fine paste. Add parmesan, season with sea salt and cracked pepper; pulse until just combined. (Makes 1¼ cups)

nutritional count per serving
121.8g total fat (21.9g saturated fat); 5852kJ (1400 cal); 31.7g carbohydrate; 39.4g protein; 6.7g fibre

tips We used a baby leaf micro herb mix of sorrel, parsley, coriander (cilantro) and radish. Leftover pesto can be stored, covered with a light layer of oil, in an airtight container in the fridge for up to 1 week.

MUSHROOM & PARMESAN
FRENCH TOAST

PREP + COOK TIME **15 MINUTES** SERVES **2**

2 FREE-RANGE EGGS
½ CUP (125ML) MILK
2 TEASPOONS DIJON MUSTARD
¼ CUP (20G) FINELY GRATED PARMESAN
4 X 2CM (¾-INCH) THICK SLICES SOURDOUGH BREAD
⅓ CUP (80ML) OLIVE OIL
300G (9½ OUNCES) BUTTON MUSHROOMS, SLICED THINLY
1 CLOVE GARLIC, CRUSHED
2 TABLESPOONS FRESH THYME LEAVES
2 TEASPOONS APPLE CIDER VINEGAR
10G (½ OUNCE) BUTTER
¼ CUP (60G) CRÈME FRAÎCHE
¼ CUP (20G) FLAKED PARMESAN
1 TABLESPOON FINELY CHOPPED FRESH CHIVES

1 Using a fork, whisk eggs, milk, mustard and grated parmesan in a shallow dish until combined; season. Soak bread slices in egg mixture for 5 minutes, turning halfway through.
2 Meanwhile, heat 1½ tablespoons of the oil in a large frying pan over medium-high heat; cook half the mushrooms, without stirring, for 1 minute or until browned underneath. Cook, stirring, a further 2 minutes or until tender. Transfer to a heatproof dish; cover with foil. Repeat process with another 1½ tablespoons of the oil and remaining mushrooms, adding garlic and thyme during the last minute of cooking; stir in vinegar and half the butter. Combine all mushrooms in dish; cover to keep warm.

3 In same cleaned pan, heat remaining oil and remaining butter over medium heat; cook bread for 2 minutes each side or until golden.
4 Serve french toast topped with mushroom mixture, crème fraîche, flaked parmesan and chives.

nutritional count per serving
65.4g total fat (23.3g saturated fat); 3482kJ (833 cal); 32.8g carbohydrate; 27.7g protein; 4.4g fibre

SUPER SEED BOWL
WITH APPLE & YOGHURT

PREP + COOK TIME **10 MINUTES** SERVES **2**

2 MEDIUM GREEN APPLES (300G), CUT INTO MATCHSTICKS

2 TABLESPOONS LEMON JUICE

½ CUP (125ML) COCONUT WATER

100G (3 OUNCES) STRAWBERRIES, SLICED THICKLY

½ CUP (140G) GREEK-STYLE YOGHURT

2 TABLESPOONS RAW HONEY

SUPER SEED MIX

2 TABLESPOONS SUNFLOWER SEEDS

2 TABLESPOONS PEPITAS (PUMPKIN SEEDS)

1½ TABLESPOONS SESAME SEEDS

1½ TABLESPOONS POPPY SEEDS

1½ TABLESPOONS CHIA SEEDS

1½ TABLESPOONS LINSEEDS (FLAXSEEDS)

2 TABLESPOONS CURRANTS

2 TABLESPOONS GOJI BERRIES

1 Make super seed mix.

2 Combine apple and juice in a medium bowl.

3 Divide apple mixture and half the seed mix between two bowls, add coconut water. Top with strawberries and yoghurt; drizzle with honey and sprinkle with remaining seed mix.

super seed mix Stir sunflower seeds and pepitas in a small frying pan over medium heat for 2 minutes or until lightly golden. Add sesame seeds, poppy seeds, chia seeds and linseeds; stir for 30 seconds or until all are toasted. Remove from pan; cool. Stir in currants and goji berries. (Makes 1 cup)

nutritional count per serving

31.2g total fat (6.2g saturated fat); 2596kJ (621 cal); 65.9g carbohydrate; 18.1g protein; 9.4g fibre

tips When in season, use pears instead of apples. Super seed mix can be made ahead. Store in an airtight container or jar in the fridge for up to 3 months.

SEEDAHOLIC BREAD WITH
ALMOND BUTTER & PEAR

PREP + COOK TIME **2 HOURS 30 MINUTES (+ STANDING & COOLING)** SERVES **2 (MAKES 10 SLICES)**

Psyllium husks are available from vitamin and health food stores.

1½ CUPS (135G) ROLLED OATS
1½ CUPS (120G) QUINOA FLAKES
1 CUP (150G) SUNFLOWER SEEDS
1 CUP (200G) PEPITAS (PUMPKIN SEEDS)
⅔ CUP (130G) LINSEEDS (FLAXSEEDS)
½ CUP (70G) WHITE CHIA SEEDS
½ CUP (80G) COARSELY CHOPPED ALMOND KERNELS
½ CUP (70G) COARSELY CHOPPED HAZELNUTS
½ CUP (40G) PSYLLIUM HUSKS
2 TEASPOONS SEA SALT FLAKES
3½ CUPS (875ML) WARM WATER
2 TABLESPOONS RAW HONEY
⅔ CUP (140G) COCONUT OIL, MELTED
¼ CUP (65G) ALMOND BUTTER
1 MEDIUM PACKHAM PEAR (250G), SLICED THINLY
1 TABLESPOON OLIVE OIL

1 Grease a 1.5-litre (6-cup), 14cm x 24cm (5½-inch x 9½-inch) loaf pan; line the base and two long sides with baking paper, extending the paper over the edge.

2 Place dry ingredients in a large bowl. Place the water, honey and coconut oil in a large jug; stir until dissolved. Pour over dry ingredients; stir to combine. (The mixture will be firm, if it is too stiff add extra tablespoons of water, one at a time.)

3 Spoon seed mixture into pan; shape with your hands into a loaf shape. Cover surface with plastic wrap; stand at room temperature for 2 hours to allow ingredients to absorb the liquid and set the bread into shape.

4 Preheat oven 200°C/400°F.

5 Bake bread for 30 minutes. Invert bread onto a wire rack on an oven tray; peel away lining paper. Return bread to oven on tray; bake a further 1 hour 20 minutes (see tips) or until a skewer inserted into the centre comes out clean. Leave 3 hours or until completely cool before slicing.

6 To serve, spread 4 slices of seedaholic bread with almond butter, top with pear slices; drizzle with olive oil. Divide between two serving plates.

nutritional count per serving
122.8g total fat (37.2g saturated fat); 6726kJ (1609 cal); 77.2g carbohydrate; 44.8g protein; 18.3g fibre

nutritional count per slice (bread only) 48.7g total fat (16.9g saturated fat); 2646kJ (633 cal); 28.6g carbohydrate; 18.7g protein; 7.3g fibre

tips Position the shelf in the oven so the top of the bread sits in the middle of the oven. If the bread starts to overbrown during baking, cover it loosely with foil. Bread will keep in an airtight container in the fridge for up to 2 weeks. Freeze individual slices in zip-top bags for up to 1 month.

EXERCISE WITH YOUR KIDS.
CHILDREN LEARN MORE FROM WHAT
YOU DO THAN WHAT YOU TEACH.

GRAIN-FREE COCONUT &
VANILLA MUESLI

PREP + COOK TIME **30 MINUTES (+ COOLING)** SERVES **4 (MAKES 4¾ CUPS)**

2 VANILLA BEANS
2½ CUPS (125G) FLAKED COCONUT
½ CUP (80G) NATURAL ALMONDS, CHOPPED COARSELY
½ CUP (80G) BRAZIL NUTS, CHOPPED COARSELY
½ CUP (60G) PECANS, CHOPPED COARSELY
¼ CUP (35G) SUNFLOWER SEEDS
½ CUP (100G) VIRGIN COCONUT OIL, MELTED
2 TABLESPOONS RAW HONEY
½ TEASPOON SEA SALT

1 Preheat oven to 160°C/300°F. Grease and line two large oven trays with baking paper.
2 Split vanilla beans in half lengthways; scrape out seeds. Place seeds and pods in a large bowl with remaining ingredients; stir to combine. Spread mixture evenly between trays.
3 Bake muesli for 20 minutes, stirring occasionally to break into clumps, or until lightly golden. Cool.

nutritional count per serving
88.8g total fat (49g saturated fat); 3916kJ (935 cal); 21.5g carbohydrate; 12.6g protein; 5.6g fibre

tip Store muesli in an airtight container in the fridge for up to 4 weeks.

serving suggestion Serve with milk or yoghurt.

PAPAYA & MACADAMIAS
WITH VEGAN YOGHURT

PREP + COOK TIME **20 MINUTES (+ STANDING)** SERVES **2**

You will need to start this recipe at least 4 hours ahead.

1 SMALL PAPAYA (650G)

¼ CUP (35G) ROASTED MACADAMIA HALVES

⅓ CUP (15G) COCONUT FLAKES, TOASTED

2 TEASPOONS FINELY GRATED LIME RIND (SEE TIPS)

2 LIMES (180G), CUT INTO WEDGES

VEGAN YOGHURT

1 CUP (150G) CASHEWS

1 CUP (160G) WHOLE BLANCHED ALMONDS

1 CUP (250ML) WATER

1 Make vegan yoghurt.

2 Cut papaya in half lengthways; scoop out the seeds.

3 Spoon 1 cup of the yoghurt into papaya hollows; sprinkle with macadamias, coconut and rind. Serve with lime wedges.

vegan yoghurt Place nuts in a large bowl with enough cold water to cover. Stand, covered, for 4 hours or overnight. Drain; rinse under cold water. Drain. Process nuts and the water until it forms a yoghurt-like consistency. (Makes 2½ cups)

nutritional count per serving
50.9g total fat (9.4g saturated fat); 2621kJ (627 cal); 23.6g carbohydrate; 14.4g protein; 12.2g fibre

tips If you have one, use a zester to cut the lime rind into long thin strips. You can experiment with different nuts to create the yoghurt, bearing in mind the flavour each nut will create. Store leftover yoghurt in the fridge for up to 1 week.

NATURAL
FACIALS

CUCUMBER COOLING MASK

Process 20 small seedless red grapes, ½ medium seeded and coarsely chopped cucumber and 3 halved strawberries until combined. Place a large piece of muslin, folded in quarters, in a small bowl. Spoon mixture into centre of cloth; gather corners of cloth and squeeze liquid from mixture into bowl; discard liquid. Place fruit pulp into a cleaned bowl; stir in 1 tablespoon natural yoghurt and ½ teaspoon honey. Apply mask, to a clean, dry face, avoiding eye and lip area. Relax for 15 minutes. Gently remove mask with a warm face cloth; rinse with warm water.

kiwifruit & lime toner

PROCESS 2 PEELED AND COARSELY CHOPPED KIWIFRUIT UNTIL ALMOST SMOOTH; TRANSFER TO A SMALL BOWL. STIR IN ⅓ CUP LIME JUICE. POUR FRUIT MIXTURE INTO A MUSLIN-LINED STRAINER OVER A SMALL BOWL. USING A RUBBER SPATULA, GENTLY PUSH LIQUID THROUGH. DISCARD PULP AND SEEDS. USING A COTTON BALL, APPLY TONER TO FACE AFTER CLEANSING, AVOIDING EYE AREA. RINSE FACE WITH COOL WATER; PAT DRY. STORE REMAINING TONER IN A SCREW-TOP JAR IN THE FRIDGE FOR 1 WEEK.

BANANA & AVOCADO MASK

MASH ¼ RIPE BANANA AND ¼ RIPE AVOCADO UNTIL ALMOST SMOOTH; PUSH THROUGH A SMALL SIEVE. STIR IN 1 TSP HONEY AND 3 TSP CORNFLOUR. APPLY MASK TO A CLEAN, DRY FACE, AVOIDING EYE AND LIP AREA. RELAX FOR 15 MINUTES. REMOVE WITH A WARM CLOTH; RINSE AND PAT DRY.

GRAPE TONER

Rub the cut-sides of halved seedless green grapes over facial and neck lines. Leave for 30 minutes before washing off with warm water. The grapes contain glycolic acid and this acts like an exfoliant, reduces oil and helps build collagen.

ALMOND & PAPAYA FACIAL SCRUB Process ¼ cup blanched almonds until they resemble fine breadcrumbs; transfer to a small bowl. Stir in ⅓ cup oat bran, 1 teaspoon sweet almond oil, 2 tablespoons pureed papaya, 1 tablespoon natural yoghurt and 2 tablespoons honey. Apply a small amount to damp cleansed face, avoiding eye area. Rinse off with warm water. Refrigerate remaining scrub for 1 week.

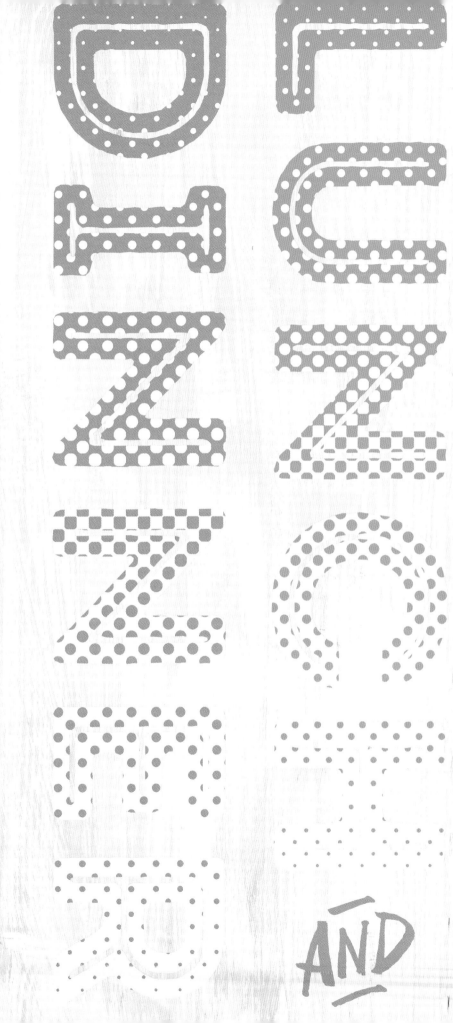

GLUTEN-FREE BREAD

PREP + COOK TIME **1 HOUR 30 MINUTES (+ STANDING)**   MAKES **1 LOAF (12 SLICES)**

This bread is best eaten the day it is baked, however, it's great for toast or toasted sandwiches the next day.

3 CUPS (405G) GLUTEN-FREE PLAIN (ALL-PURPOSE) FLOUR
½ CUP (75G) POTATO FLOUR
½ CUP (80G) BROWN RICE FLOUR
½ CUP (80G) WHITE RICE FLOUR
3 TEASPOONS (10G) DRIED YEAST
2 TEASPOONS SALT
2 TEASPOONS XANTHAN GUM
1 EGG
3 EGG WHITES
¾ CUP (180ML) OLIVE OIL
1 TEASPOON VINEGAR
2 CUPS (500ML) WARM WATER
1 TABLESPOON OLIVE OIL, EXTRA
2 TEASPOONS SALT, EXTRA

1 Grease a 12cm x 20cm (4¾-inch x 8-inch) loaf pan; lightly dust with rice flour.

2 Combine sifted flours, yeast, salt and gum in a large bowl.

3 Place egg, egg whites, oil, vinegar and 1½ cups of the water in a large bowl of an electric mixer; beat on medium speed for 3½ minutes. Add remaining water and the flour mixture, 1 cup at a time, beating until combined and smooth.

4 Spoon mixture into loaf pan; smooth the surface. Cover; stand in a warm place for 45 minutes.

5 Preheat oven to 220°C/425°F.

6 Drizzle loaf with extra oil and sprinkle with extra salt. Bake for 1 hour or until crust is firm and golden brown and the loaf sounds hollow when tapped. Stand bread in pan for 5 minutes before turning, top-side up, onto a wire rack to cool.

nutritional count per slice

16.1g total fat (2.4g saturated fat); 1400kJ (335 cal); 43.8g carbohydrate; 3g protein; 0.7g fibre

tip This gluten-free bread mixture will make 6 rolls. Divide the dough into 6 even portions, roll into balls and place on a greased and floured (rice flour) oven tray. Stand for 45 minutes. Drizzle rolls with oil and sprinkle with salt; bake for 30 minutes.

SMOKED TROUT &
AVOCADO ROLLS

- - - - - - - - -

RECIPE PAGE 100

CHICKEN & ROAST
PUMPKIN ROLLS

- - - - - - - - -

RECIPE PAGE 100

MUSHROOM &
LABNE ROLLS
- - - - - - - - - -
RECIPE PAGE 100

MIDDLE-EASTERN
EGG SANDWICHES
- - - - - - - - - -
RECIPE PAGE 100

SMOKED TROUT & AVOCADO ROLLS

PREP TIME **10 MINUTES** SERVES **2**

Cut a lebanese cucumber in half crossways; cut one half into ribbons using a vegetable peeler. Coarsely grate remaining cucumber and squeeze out excess moisture; combine grated cucumber in a bowl with 2 tablespoons low-fat plain yoghurt and 1 teaspoon ground fennel. Cut 2 bread rolls (or soy and linseed sourdough) in half; toast cut sides. Divide half a small sliced avocado, 60g (2oz) sliced smoked ocean trout and 1 teaspoon dill sprigs evenly between roll bases. Top roll tops evenly with the cucumber ribbons and cucumber yoghurt mixture. Sandwich bread rolls together to serve.

tip If ground fennel is unavailable, grind the fennel seeds in a mortar and pestle or a mini food processor.

(photograph page 98)

MUSHROOM & LABNE ROLLS

PREP + COOK TIME **15 MINUTES** SERVES **2**

Roughly chop 80g (2½oz) each of swiss brown and button mushrooms. Lightly spray a large frying pan with cooking oil. Cook mushrooms, 1 crushed garlic clove and 2 teaspoons fresh thyme leaves, over medium heat, for 5 minutes or until browned. Cut 2 seeded sourdough rolls in half; toast cut sides. Divide 3 tablespoons labne and the mushroom mixture evenly between roll bases; evenly drizzle with 2 teaspoons of olive oil. Top roll tops with 2 radicchio leaves each. Sandwich bread rolls together to serve.

tip Labne is a cheese made from strained yoghurt. You can find it in supermarkets.

(photograph page 99)

CHICKEN & ROAST PUMPKIN ROLLS

PREP + COOK TIME **30 MINUTES** SERVES **2**

Preheat oven to 220°C/425°F. Line an oven tray with baking paper. Place 200g (6½oz) coarsely chopped pumpkin onto tray. Spray with cooking oil and sprinkle with 1 teaspoon dukkah. Bake for 25 minutes or until tender; mash roughly with a fork. Cut 2 bread rolls (or wholemeal sourdough) in half; toast cut sides. Divide pumpkin and 1 tablespoon radish sprouts evenly between roll bases. Combine 1 teaspoon macadamia oil and ½ teaspoon dukkah and drizzle evenly over sprouts. Top roll tops evenly with 20g (¾oz) baby spinach leaves and 125g (4oz) sliced smoked chicken breast. Sandwich bread rolls together to serve.

(photograph page 98)

MIDDLE-EASTERN EGG SANDWICHES

PREP TIME **10 MINUTES** SERVES **2**

Mash 2 extra large hard-boiled eggs with a fork in a medium bowl. Stir in ¼ cup reduced-fat cottage cheese and 1 tablespoon pistachio dukkah. Divide ¼ thinly sliced small red onion, egg mixture and 2 teaspoons micro cress evenly over 2 slices of toasted rye sourdough. Divide 25g (¾oz) watercress sprigs between another 2 slices toasted rye sourdough. Sandwich bread slices together to serve.

tips Pistachio dukkah is available from most major supermarkets in the spice aisle. Store remaining watercress in the fridge with its stems in water, like flowers, for 2 days.

(photograph page 99)

TUNA & QUINOA TABBOULEH ROLLS

PREP + COOK TIME **25 MINUTES (+ COOLING)**

SERVES **2**

Bring ¼ cup rinsed, drained quinoa and ¾ cup of water to the boil in a small saucepan over high heat. Reduce heat to low; cook, covered, for 15 minutes or until liquid is absorbed. Cool. Place quinoa in a small bowl with 1 finely chopped tomato, 1 finely sliced green onion (scallion), 2 tablespoons each of coarsely chopped fresh flat-leaf parsley and mint, 1 tablespoon olive oil and 1½ tablespoons lemon juice; stir to combine. Season. Cut 2 bread rolls in half; spread half a mashed avocado between roll bases. Divide 95g (3oz) canned drained flaked tuna over avocado and top with 1 tablespoon radish sprouts. Top roll tops with quinoa tabbouleh. Sandwich bread rolls together to serve.

tip Use poached chicken breast or salmon instead of tuna.

(photograph page 102)

PASTRAMI & SILVER BEET SLAW ROLLS

PREP TIME **15 MINUTES** SERVES **2**

To make silver beet coleslaw, cut 1 medium carrot into matchsticks; combine in a medium bowl with 2 finely shredded medium silver beet leaves, 1 thinly sliced green onion (scallion), 2 tablespoons plain soy yoghurt and 1½ teaspoons dijon mustard. Season to taste. Cut 2 bread rolls in half. Spoon silver beet coleslaw equally between roll bases. Top each roll top with 50g (1½oz) pastrami slices. Sandwich bread rolls together to serve.

tip Use roast beef slices instead of the pastrami.

(photograph page 102)

CHAR-GRILLED VEGIE ROLLS

PREP TIME **15 MINUTES** SERVES **2**

Drain 280g (9oz) jar of char-grilled vegetables; pat dry on paper towel, season to taste. Cut 2 bread rolls in half. Spread ⅓ cup moroccan pumpkin dip evenly over roll bases; top equally with char-grilled vegetables. Divide 20g (¾oz) baby rocket leaves between roll tops. Sandwich bread rolls together to serve.

tip Leftover pumpkin dip can be eaten with crackers.

(photograph page 103)

CHICKEN & AVOCADO ROLLS

PREP TIME **20 MINUTES** SERVES **2**

Combine 1 cup sliced cooked chicken, ⅓ cup coarsely chopped fresh coriander, 2 tablespoons coarsely chopped fresh mint, 2 teaspoons finely grated lemon rind and 1 tablespoon each of lemon juice and grapeseed oil in a small bowl; season. Cut two rolls in half. Spoon chicken mixture equally over roll bases. Top roll tops evenly with ½ medium thinly sliced avocado and 1 each medium lebanese cucumber and carrot sliced into ribbons. Sandwich bread rolls together to serve.

tips Use a vegetable peeler to cut carrot and cucumber into ribbons. We used skinless barbecue chicken breasts.

(photograph page 103)

TUNA & QUINOA
TABBOULEH ROLLS
- - - - - - - - - -
RECIPE PAGE 101

PASTRAMI & SILVER
BEET SLAW ROLLS
- - - - - - - - - -
RECIPE PAGE 101

CHAR-GRILLED
VEGIE ROLLS
- - - - - - - - -
RECIPE PAGE 101

CHICKEN &
AVOCADO ROLLS
- - - - - - - - -
RECIPE PAGE 101

QUINOA, ZUCCHINI & FETTA SALAD

PREP + COOK TIME **35 MINUTES** SERVES **4**

¾ CUP (150G) WHITE QUINOA

1½ CUPS (375ML) WATER

½ CUP (70G) HAZELNUTS

2 MEDIUM ZUCCHINI (240G),
   CUT INTO LONG THIN STRIPS

250G (8 OUNCES) HEIRLOOM OR
   MIXED CHERRY TOMATOES,
   HALVED

½ SMALL RED ONION (50G),
   SLICED THINLY

100G (3 OUNCES) FETTA,
   CRUMBLED

1 CUP LOOSELY PACKED FRESH
   SMALL BASIL LEAVES

2 TABLESPOONS EXTRA VIRGIN
   OLIVE OIL

1 TABLESPOON RED WINE
   VINEGAR

1 Rinse quinoa under cold water; drain well. Place in a medium saucepan with the water; bring to the boil. Reduce heat; simmer, covered, for 15 minutes or until water is absorbed and quinoa is tender. Transfer to a large serving bowl to cool.

2 Meanwhile, roast hazelnuts in a medium frying pan over medium heat for 4 minutes or until golden. Rub hot hazelnuts in a clean tea towel to remove most of the skin; discard skin. Coarsely chop nuts.

3 Add nuts to quinoa in bowl with zucchini, tomatoes, onion, half the fetta and half the basil. Drizzle with combined oil and vinegar; toss gently to combine. Season to taste. Serve topped with remaining fetta and remaining basil, sprinkled with pepper.

nutritional count per serving
28g total fat (5.9g saturated fat); 1791kJ (428 cal); 27.6g carbohydrate; 13.2g protein; 6g fibre

tip Use a julienne peeler, mandoline or V-slicer to cut the zucchini into long thin strips, or coarsely grate it instead, if you prefer.

serving suggestion Serve with steamed asparagus and bread.

SPICED FREEKEH & CUCUMBER

WITH GARLIC MINT YOGHURT

PREP + COOK TIME **45 MINUTES** SERVES **6**

2 TABLESPOONS OLIVE OIL

1 LARGE BROWN ONION (200G), CHOPPED FINELY

2 CLOVES GARLIC, CRUSHED

2 MEDIUM CARROTS (240G), DICED INTO SMALL CUBES

1 TEASPOON GROUND ALLSPICE

1 TEASPOON GROUND CORIANDER

½ TEASPOON CHILLI POWDER

2 TEASPOONS CUMIN SEEDS

1½ CUPS (300G) CRACKED GREEN WHEAT FREEKEH

1 BAY LEAF

2½ CUPS (625ML) VEGETABLE STOCK OR WATER

2 LEBANESE CUCUMBERS (260G)

1 FRESH LONG GREEN CHILLI, SLICED THINLY

½ CUP FRESH CORIANDER (CILANTRO) LEAVES

½ CUP (80G) FLAKED ALMONDS, ROASTED

GARLIC MINT YOGHURT

1½ CUPS (420G) GREEK-STYLE YOGHURT

2 CLOVES GARLIC, CRUSHED

¼ CUP LIGHTLY PACKED FINELY CHOPPED FRESH MINT

1 Heat oil in a large saucepan over medium heat; cook onion, garlic and carrot, stirring, for 3 minutes. Add spices and seeds; cook, stirring, for 2 minutes. Stir in freekeh to coat. Add bay leaf and stock; bring to the boil. Reduce heat to low; cook, covered, for 20 minutes or until most of the liquid is absorbed. Remove from heat; stand, covered, for 10 minutes.

2 Meanwhile, make garlic mint yoghurt.

3 Using a vegetable peeler, peel cucumbers lengthways into long thin ribbons.

4 Serve freekeh mixture topped with yoghurt, cucumber and combined chilli, coriander and nuts.

garlic mint yoghurt Combine ingredients in a small bowl; season to taste.

nutritional count per serving

19.4g total fat (4.3g saturated fat); 1886kJ (450 cal); 52g carbohydrate; 14.9g protein; 12.9g fibre

tips Freekeh is roasted green wheat that contains more nutrients than the mature version of the same grain. It has a delicious nutty taste and texture, and is available from most major supermarkets and health food stores. If you prefer, use ground cinnamon instead of the allspice.

BEEF & WOMBOK
HERB SALAD

PREP + COOK TIME **15 MINUTES** SERVES **4**

1 TABLESPOON VEGETABLE OIL

300G (9½ OUNCES) BEEF
STIR-FRY STRIPS

½ SMALL WOMBOK (NAPA
CABBAGE) (350G),
SHREDDED FINELY

1 FRESH LONG RED CHILLI,
SLICED THINLY

¾ CUP (105G) ROASTED PEANUTS,
CHOPPED COARSELY

100G (3 OUNCES) BABY
SPINACH LEAVES

1½ CUPS LOOSELY PACKED
FRESH MINT LEAVES

½ CUP LOOSELY PACKED FRESH
VIETNAMESE MINT LEAVES

TAMARIND DRESSING

1½ TABLESPOONS TAMARIND
PUREE

½ CUP (175G) RICE MALT SYRUP
(SEE TIPS)

2 TABLESPOONS LIME JUICE

2 TABLESPOONS FISH SAUCE

1 Make tamarind dressing.

2 Heat oil in a wok over high heat; stir-fry beef for 3 minutes or until cooked through.

3 Place beef in a large bowl with wombok, chilli, peanuts, spinach, herbs and dressing; toss to combine.

tamarind dressing Whisk ingredients in a small bowl until combined.

nutritional count per serving

19g total fat (2.6g saturated fat); 1904kJ (455 cal); 41.3g carbohydrate; 28.3g protein; 7g fibre

tips Rice malt syrup is also known as brown rice syrup. It is available in the health food section in most supermarkets. If you prefer, use prawns, chicken or tofu instead of the beef strips.

MAPLE & DIJON

PREP TIME **5 MINUTES**   MAKES **⅔ CUP**

Whisk ¼ cup macadamia oil, ¼ cup apple cider vinegar, 2 tablespoons pure maple syrup and 1 tablespoon dijon mustard in a small bowl until combined. Season to taste.

tips Use olive oil instead macadamia oil. Store in a sealed jar in the fridge for up to 1 month. Serve with a mixed leaf salad, or beef and beetroot, or chicken and haloumi, or lamb and roast sweet potato.

HEALTHY CAESAR

PREP TIME **5 MINUTES**   MAKES **1 CUP**

Blend or process 1 cup yoghurt, 2 tablespoons olive oil, 2 tablespoons finely grated parmesan, 4 finely chopped anchovies, ½ crushed garlic clove, 1 tablespoon lemon juice and 3 teaspoons dijon mustard until smooth. Season to taste.

tips Store in a sealed jar in the fridge for up to 1 week. Serve with a caesar salad

SUGAR FREE DRESSINGS

NATURAL SWEET

SMOOTH CREAMY

AVOCADO, LEMON & DILL

PREP TIME **10 MINUTES**   MAKES **1½ CUPS**

Blend or process 1 medium (250g) avocado, ¼ cup yoghurt,
2 tablespoons avocado oil, ⅓ cup water, ⅓ cup loosely
packed fresh dill sprigs and ¼ cup of lemon juice until
smooth. Season to taste. For a thinner consistency,
add a little more water if necessary.

*tips Store in a sealed jar in the fridge for up
to 1 week. Serve with a salad of iceberg lettuce
and soft-boiled egg, or poached chicken and
pistachio, or smoked salmon.*

RASPBERRY & WHITE BALSAMIC

PREP TIME **5 MINUTES**   MAKES **½ CUP**

Push ½ cup fresh or thawed frozen raspberries through
a fine sieve into a small bowl, using the back of a spoon.
Whisk in ¼ cup white balsamic vinegar, 2 tablespoons
macadamia oil and 1 teaspoon norbu (monk fruit sugar)
or stevia granules. Season to taste.

*tips Store in a sealed jar in the fridge for up
to 1 week. Serve with a salad of roast duck,
slow cooked lamb or grilled chicken.*

FRESH & HERBAL

FRUITY & NUTTY

FENNEL, APPLE & PISTACHIO
CHICKEN SALAD

PREP + COOK TIME **25 MINUTES (+ COOLING)** SERVES **4**

2 CUPS (500ML) CHICKEN STOCK

2 CUPS (500ML) WATER

4 THIN SLICES LEMON

4 CLOVES GARLIC, BRUISED (SEE TIPS)

6 FRESH THYME SPRIGS

2 X 200G (6½-OUNCE) FREE-RANGE CHICKEN BREASTS

½ CUP (125ML) LEMON JUICE

1 TABLESPOON DIJON MUSTARD

⅓ CUP (80ML) EXTRA VIRGIN OLIVE OIL

1 SMALL FENNEL (130G), SLICED THINLY

1 MEDIUM APPLE (150G), SLICED THINLY

1 CUP (40G) TRIMMED WATERCRESS

1 CUP FIRMLY PACKED FRESH FLAT-LEAF PARSLEY LEAVES

1 CUP FIRMLY PACKED TORN FRESH MINT

1 MEDIUM AVOCADO (250G), SLICED THINLY

½ CUP (60G) PISTACHIOS, CHOPPED COARSELY

1 Place stock, the water, lemon slices, garlic and thyme in a medium saucepan over medium heat. Add chicken; bring to the boil. Reduce heat; simmer for 4 minutes. Cover pan, turn off heat; set aside to cool to room temperature. Remove chicken; shred coarsely. (Reserve poaching liquid for another use; see tips.)

2 Whisk juice and mustard together in a small bowl until combined; gradually whisk in oil until combined. Season to taste.

3 Place fennel, apple, watercress, herbs and avocado in a large bowl. Add chicken and dressing; toss to combine. Season to taste. Serve salad topped with pistachios.

nutritional count per serving
41.7g total fat (7.7g saturated fat); 2268kJ (542 cal); 11g carbohydrate; 28g protein; 7.2g fibre

tips To bruise garlic, place the flat side of a cook's knife on the unpeeled clove; using the heel of your other hand push down on the knife to flatten it. Remove the skin. When poaching chicken, it is easy to overcook it and make it tough. The secret to keeping it tender and moist, is to finish off the cooking in the gentle residual heat of the pan. This method also works well with fish. Store the reserved poaching liquid in the fridge for up to 3 days.

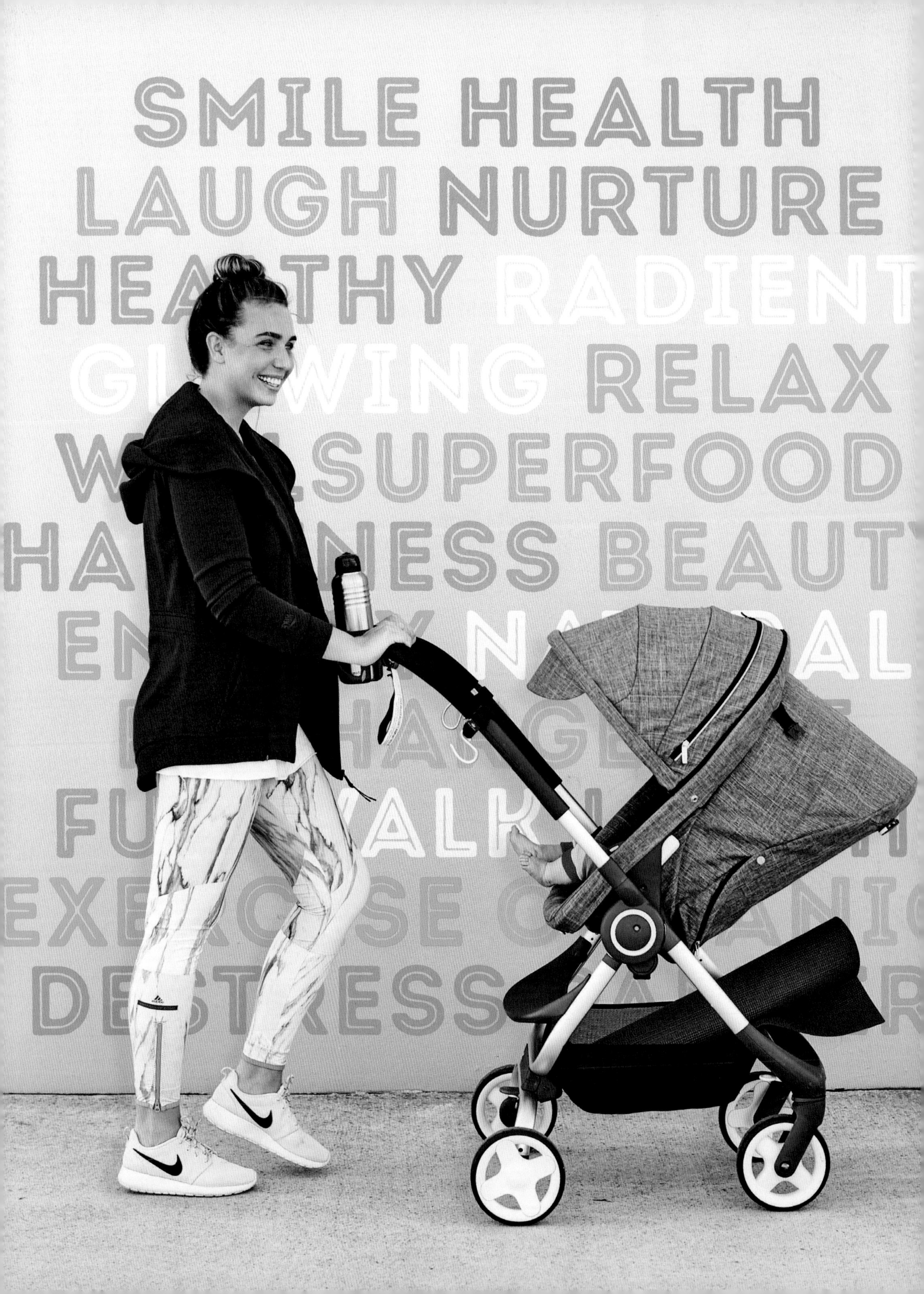
SMILE HEALTH
LAUGH NURTURE
RADIENT
RELAX
SUPERFOOD

A GREAT WAY TO GET FUSSY LITTLE
EATERS TO EAT THEIR GREENS IS BY
BLENDING THEM INTO A SMOOTHIE OR
A JUICE. SERVE IT IN A GLASS JAR
OR THEIR FAVOURITE CUP WITH A
COLOURFUL STRAW TO MAKE IT FUN!

KALE
CAESAR SALAD

PREP + COOK TIME **45 MINUTES (+ COOLING)** SERVES **4**

1 LITRE (4 CUPS) WATER

4 SPRIGS FRESH THYME

2 CLOVES GARLIC, CRUSHED

½ MEDIUM LEMON (70G), SLICED THINLY

400G (12½ OUNCES) FREE-RANGE CHICKEN BREAST FILLETS

12 THIN SLICES SOURDOUGH BAGUETTE (100G)

¾ CUP (60G) FINELY GRATED PARMESAN

1 TABLESPOON OLIVE OIL

8 FREE-RANGE MIDDLE BACON SLICES (240G)

1 TEASPOON WHITE VINEGAR

4 FREE-RANGE EGGS

240G (7½ OUNCES) BABY KALE LEAVES

GREEN GODDESS DRESSING

¼ CUP (75G) WHOLE-EGG MAYONNAISE

2 TABLESPOONS SOUR CREAM

¼ CUP COARSELY CHOPPED FRESH FLAT-LEAF PARSLEY

1 TABLESPOON COARSELY CHOPPED FRESH BASIL

1 TABLESPOON COARSELY CHOPPED FRESH CHIVES

2 TABLESPOONS WATER

1 TABLESPOON LEMON JUICE

1 DRAINED ANCHOVY FILLET, CHOPPED COARSELY

1 CLOVE GARLIC, CHOPPED FINELY

1 Bring the water, thyme sprigs, garlic and lemon to the boil in a medium saucepan. Add chicken, return to the boil. Reduce heat; simmer, uncovered, for 12 minutes or until chicken is cooked through. Remove chicken; cool 10 minutes, then shred coarsely. Reserve poaching liquid for another use (see tips).

2 Meanwhile, make green goddess dressing.

3 Preheat grill (broiler). Toast bread on one side, then turn and sprinkle with half the parmesan; grill croûtons until parmesan melts and is browned lightly.

4 Heat oil in a small frying pan over medium heat, cook bacon until golden and crisp; drain on paper towel.

5 Half fill a large saucepan with water; bring to the boil. Add vinegar to water. Break one 1 egg into a cup then slide into pan; repeat with remaining eggs. When eggs are in pan, return to the boil. Cover pan, turn off heat; stand 3 minutes or until a light film of egg white sets over the yolks.

6 Meanwhile, place kale and one-quarter of the dressing in a large bowl; toss to combine. Stand for 5 minutes to soften slightly.

7 Add croûtons, bacon, remaining parmesan and dressing; toss to combine. Serve salad topped with poached egg.

green goddess dressing Process ingredients until smooth and combined; season. (Makes ¾ cup)

nutritional count per serving

43.6g total fat (12.9g saturated fat); 2759kJ (660 cal); 15.2g carbohydrate; 51.3g protein; 2.8g fibre

tip The poaching liquid in step 1 can be used as a light chicken stock for any other recipe using chicken stock. Allow to cool; refrigerate and use within 2 days, or freeze up to 1 month.

BEETROOT, BLOOD ORANGE & PORK SALAD

PREP + COOK TIME **40 MINUTES** SERVES **4**

1 WHOLEMEAL BAGUETTE (240G)

2 TABLESPOONS OLIVE OIL

200G (6½ OUNCES) FREE-RANGE PORK FILLET, TRIMMED

440G (14 OUNCES) CANNED BABY BEETROOTS (BEETS), HALVED

3 SMALL BLOOD ORANGES (570G), PEELED, SLICED THINLY

100G (3 OUNCES) RADICCHIO LEAVES, TORN

75G (2½ OUNCES) MESCLUN SALAD LEAVES

8 FRESH PITTED DATES (160G), HALVED

½ CUP (60G) PITTED KALAMATA OLIVES, HALVED

2 TABLESPOONS PEPITAS (PUMPKIN SEEDS), ROASTED

2 TABLESPOONS SUNFLOWER SEEDS, ROASTED

2 TEASPOONS POPPY SEEDS

RASPBERRY DRESSING

2 TABLESPOONS RASPBERRY WINE VINEGAR

2 TABLESPOONS OLIVE OIL

1 TABLESPOON ORANGE BLOSSOM WATER

1 CLOVE GARLIC, CRUSHED

2 TEASPOONS CHOPPED FRESH CHIVES

1 Make raspberry dressing.

2 Cut baguette in half horizontally, then in half crossways. Drizzle oil on baguette pieces and pork; season.

3 Cook pork on a lightly oiled heated grill plate (or grill or barbecue), turning frequently, for 15 minutes or until cooked through. Rest for 5 minutes; slice thickly.

4 Place bread pieces, cut-side down, on the oiled heated grill plate for 2 minutes each side or until golden. Tear bread into large pieces.

5 Place pork in a large bowl with beetroot, blood oranges, radicchio, mesclun, dates, olives and dressing; toss to gently combine. Sprinkle salad with seeds, serve with bread.

raspberry dressing Combine ingredients in a small bowl; season to taste.

nutritional count per serving

27.8g total fat (4.3g saturated fat); 2709kJ (648 cal); 69.1g carbohydrate; 24.4g protein; 14.3g fibre

tip You can use grilled chicken breast or thigh fillets instead of the pork, if you like.

TUNA SALAD
SUSHI BOWL

PREP + COOK TIME **35 MINUTES** SERVES **4**

⅓ CUP (80ML) TERIYAKI SAUCE

⅓ CUP (80ML) RICE VINEGAR

1 TABLESPOON FINELY GRATED
   FRESH GINGER

450G (14½ OUNCES) PACKAGED
   BROWN MICROWAVE RICE

2 X 185G (6 OUNCES) CANNED
   TUNA IN SPRINGWATER,
   DRAINED

1 LEBANESE CUCUMBER (130G),
   HALVED LENGTHWAYS,
   SEEDED, SLICED THINLY
   LENGTHWAYS

1 LARGE AVOCADO (320G),
   SLICED THINLY

1 LARGE CARROT (180G),
   CUT INTO MATCHSTICKS

⅓ CUP (90G) DRAINED PICKLED
   GINGER, SLICED THINLY

1 TABLESPOON SESAME SEEDS,
   TOASTED

½ SHEET TOASTED SEAWEED
   (NORI), SHREDDED FINELY

1 Combine sauce, vinegar and ginger in a small bowl.

2 Reheat rice following packet instructions.

3 Combine warm rice and half the dressing in a bowl.

4 Serve rice with tuna, cucumber, avocado, carrot and pickled ginger. Drizzle with remaining dressing; sprinkle with sesame seeds and seaweed.

nutritional count per serving

16.7g total fat (3.7g saturated fat); 1793kJ (429 cal); 40.4g carbohydrate; 24.8g protein; 6g fibre

tip Use tamari instead of teriyaki sauce, if you prefer.

GREEN GOODNESS
IN A BOWL

PREP + COOK TIME **20 MINUTES** SERVES **4**

150G (4½ OUNCES) SNOW PEAS, TRIMMED

200G (6½ OUNCES) GREEN BEANS, TRIMMED, HALVED LENGTHWAYS

200G (6½ OUNCES) BROCCOLINI, HALVED ON THE DIAGONAL

2 TEASPOONS OLIVE OIL

500G (1 POUND) PACKAGED BROWN MICROWAVE RICE

2 TABLESPOONS PEPITAS (PUMPKIN SEEDS), TOASTED, CHOPPED COARSELY

1 MEDIUM AVOCADO (250G), SLICED THINLY

1 TABLESPOON PEPITAS (PUMPKIN SEEDS), TOASTED, EXTRA

AVOCADO YOGHURT DRESSING

1 MEDIUM AVOCADO (250G), CHOPPED COARSELY

¾ CUP (200G) GREEK-STYLE YOGHURT

¼ CUP FRESH BASIL LEAVES

2 TABLESPOONS LIME JUICE

1 SMALL CLOVE GARLIC, CHOPPED FINELY

1 TABLESPOON OLIVE OIL

1 TABLESPOON WATER

1 Make avocado yoghurt dressing.

2 Boil, steam or microwave peas, beans and broccolini, separately, until tender; drain.

3 Place peas, beans and broccolini in a large bowl with oil; toss gently to combine. Cover to keep warm.

4 Heat rice following instructions on packet. Combine rice and chopped pepitas in a medium bowl; season to taste.

5 Serve rice topped with three-quarters of the dressing, then vegetables, avocado, remaining dressing and extra pepitas.

avocado yoghurt dressing Blend or process ingredients until smooth and combined; season to taste.

nutritional count per serving
24.6g total fat (5.4g saturated fat); 2136kJ (511 cal); 53.3g carbohydrate; 13.7g protein; 5.9g fibre

tip For a spicy version, add 2 teaspoons chopped pickled jalapeños to the dressing.

SMOKED TOFU
WITH PEANUT DRESSING

PREP + COOK TIME **45 MINUTES** SERVES **4**

4 FREE-RANGE EGGS

¼ CUP (60ML) WATER

1 TABLESPOON FRIED ASIAN SHALLOTS

1 TEASPOON TAMARI

1 TABLESPOON SESAME OIL

350G (11 OUNCES) SMOKED TOFU (SEE TIP), CUT INTO 1CM (½-INCH) PIECES

1 MEDIUM AVOCADO (250G), SLICED THINLY

250G (8 OUNCES) CHERRY TOMATOES, HALVED

1½ CUP (120G) BEAN SPROUTS

½ CUP LOOSELY PACKED FRESH CORIANDER (CILANTRO) LEAVES

½ CUP LOOSELY PACKED FRESH VIETNAMESE MINT LEAVES

75G (2½ OUNCES) BABY SALAD LEAVES

2 TABLESPOONS BLACK SESAME SEEDS

PEANUT DRESSING

⅓ CUP (45G) ROASTED PEANUTS, CHOPPED COARSELY

1 GREEN ONION (SCALLION), SLICED THINLY

1 FRESH LONG RED CHILLI, SLICED THINLY

1 TEASPOON FINELY GRATED FRESH GINGER

1 CLOVE GARLIC, CRUSHED

1½ TABLESPOONS GRATED PALM SUGAR

2 TABLESPOONS SESAME OIL

2 TABLESPOONS TAMARI

¼ CUP (60ML) RICE VINEGAR

1½ TABLESPOONS LIME JUICE

1 Make peanut dressing.

2 Whisk eggs, the water, shallots and tamari in a large bowl; season.

3 Heat oil in a wok over medium heat. Pour half the egg mixture into wok; cook, tilting wok, until almost set. Remove omelette from wok. Repeat with remaining egg mixture. Roll omelettes tightly, then slice thinly; reserve.

4 Place tofu in a large bowl with remaining ingredients and peanut dressing; toss to combine.

5 Serve tofu salad topped with reserved omelette.

peanut dressing Whisk ingredients in a medium bowl until combined.

nutritional count per serving
46.1g total fat (8.3g saturated fat); 2508kJ (600 cal); 14g carbohydrate; 29.3g protein; 7.1g fibre

tip Smoked tofu is available from health food stores; use regular hard tofu instead.

ROASTED TOMATO &
WHITE BEAN
SOUP

PREP + COOK TIME **1 HOUR 10 MINUTES** SERVES **4**

1KG (2 POUNDS) RIPE ROMA (EGG) TOMATOES, QUARTERED
1 MEDIUM RED ONION (170G), CUT INTO WEDGES
6 CLOVES GARLIC, UNPEELED
1 TABLESPOON MAPLE SYRUP
½ CUP (125ML) EXTRA VIRGIN OLIVE OIL
⅓ CUP LOOSELY PACKED SAGE LEAVES
400G (12½ OUNCES) CANNED CANNELLINI BEANS, DRAINED, RINSED
2 CUPS (500ML) WATER

1 Preheat oven to 200°C/400°F.

2 Place tomatoes, onion and garlic in a roasting pan. Combine maple syrup and half the oil in a bowl, season to taste; pour over vegetables, then toss to coat. Roast for 45 minutes or until tomatoes are very soft and coloured at the edges.

3 Meanwhile, heat remaining oil in a small frying pan over medium heat; fry sage leaves, stirring for 1 minute or until crisp. Remove with a slotted spoon; drain on paper towel. Reserve sage oil.

4 Peel roasted garlic. Blend garlic, onion, two-thirds of the tomatoes and two-thirds of the beans until smooth. Pour mixture into a large saucepan with the water and remaining beans; cook over medium heat, stirring occasionally until warmed through. Season to taste.

5 Ladle soup into bowls. Top with remaining tomatoes and crisp sage leaves; drizzle with reserved sage oil.

nutritional count per serving
29g total fat (4.5g saturated fat); 1512kJ (361 cal); 19g carbohydrate; 5.7g protein; 2.1g fibre

tip Tomatoes contain the carotenoid lycopene, an antioxidant that gives them their red colour, and may be useful in reducing the risk of some cancers and heart disease. While cooking does slightly reduce the vitamin C content in tomatoes, it actually increases the lycopene content.

SPICED CARROT SOUP WITH SMOKED ALMONDS

PREP + COOK TIME **50 MINUTES** SERVES **4**

- **2 TABLESPOONS EXTRA VIRGIN OLIVE OIL**
- **2 MEDIUM BROWN ONIONS (300G), CHOPPED COARSELY**
- **20G (¾-OUNCE) PIECE FRESH GINGER, GRATED FINELY**
- **2 TEASPOONS GROUND CUMIN**
- **1 TEASPOON GROUND CORIANDER**
- **½ CINNAMON STICK**
- **1KG (2 POUNDS) CARROTS, CUT INTO 1CM (½-INCH) ROUNDS**
- **2 CUPS (500ML) VEGETABLE STOCK**
- **3 CUPS (750ML) WATER**
- **¾ CUP (200G) GREEK-STYLE YOGHURT**
- **2 CLOVES GARLIC, CRUSHED**
- **½ SMALL RED ONION (50G), SLICED THINLY**
- **¼ CUP (40G) CHOPPED SMOKED ALMONDS**
- **8 SPRIGS FRESH CORIANDER (CILANTRO)**

1 Heat oil in a large saucepan over medium heat; cook brown onion, stirring, until soft.

2 Add ginger, cumin, ground coriander and cinnamon to the pan; cook, stirring, until fragrant. Add carrot, stock and the water; bring to the boil. Reduce heat; simmer, covered, for 20 minutes or until carrot is soft. Remove cinnamon stick. Stand soup for 10 minutes.

3 Meanwhile, combine yoghurt and garlic in a small bowl.

4 Blend soup in batches until smooth (or use a stick blender). Return soup to same pan; stir over medium heat until hot. Season.

5 Ladle soup into serving bowls; top with yoghurt mixture, red onion, almonds and coriander. Sprinkle with pepper.

nutritional count per serving
19.2g total fat (4g saturated fat); 1404kJ (335 cal); 25.6g carbohydrate; 9.2g protein; 13g fibre

CAULIFLOWER BURGERS

PREP + COOK TIME **40 MINUTES (+ REFRIGERATION)** MAKES **4**

350G (11 OUNCES) BEETROOT (BEETS), PEELED, GRATED

1 SMALL RED ONION (100G), SLICED THINLY

1 TEASPOON SALT FLAKES

¼ CUP (60ML) RED WINE VINEGAR

1 TABLESPOON LIGHT BROWN SUGAR

2 TABLESPOONS CHOPPED FRESH THYME

250G (8 OUNCES) CAULIFLOWER, CHOPPED COARSELY

140G (4½-OUNCE) PIECE CHEDDAR CHEESE

½ CUP (100G) CANNED CANNELLINI BEANS, DRAINED, RINSED

1 CUP (70G) FRESH BREADCRUMBS

2 TABLESPOONS CHOPPED FRESH FLAT-LEAF PARSLEY

2 TEASPOONS FINELY GRATED LEMON RIND

2 TABLESPOONS SKINLESS CHOPPED HAZELNUTS, ROASTED

1 EGG WHITE, BEATEN LIGHTLY

2 TABLESPOONS VEGETABLE OIL

8 LARGE BUTTER (BOSTON) LETTUCE LEAVES

125G (4 OUNCES) HEIRLOOM CHERRY TOMATOES, HALVED

LEMON MAYONNAISE

⅓ CUP (100G) MAYONNAISE

2 TEASPOONS FINELY GRATED LEMON RIND

2 TEASPOONS LEMON JUICE

1 Place beetroot, onion, salt flakes, vinegar, sugar and thyme in a medium saucepan; bring to the boil. Reduce heat; simmer, uncovered, stirring occasionally, for 20 minutes or until beetroot is tender and slightly sticky. Cool.

2 Meanwhile, boil, steam or microwave cauliflower until tender; drain. Leave to cool. Thinly slice 90g (3 ounces) of the cheddar; grate remaining cheddar.

3 Place cauliflower and beans in a food processo; pulse until coarsely chopped (do not over process). Place cauliflower in a large bowl with ¼ cup (15g) of the breadcrumbs, the grated cheddar, parsley, rind and nuts; season, stir to combine. Shape cauliflower mixture into four patties. Refrigerate for 30 minutes.

4 Make lemon mayonnaise.

5 Dip patties in egg white; coat patties in remaining breadcrumbs.

6 Heat oil in a large frying pan over medium-high heat; cook patties for 4 minutes each side or until browned and crisp. Drain on paper towel. Immediately top with sliced cheese for cheese to melt.

7 Place each patty in a lettuce leaf; top with tomato and a generous spoonful of the beetroot mixture (you will only use half the mixture, see tip). Drizzle with lemon mayonnaise; top with remaining lettuce leaf.

lemon mayonnaise Whisk ingredients in a small bowl until combined; season to taste.

nutritional count per burger

35g total fat (10.8g saturated fat); 2297kJ (548 cal); 35.3g carbohydrate; 19.7g protein; 7.3g fibre

tip Refrigerate leftover beetroot mixture in an airtight container for up to 1 week.

KINGFISH CEVICHE TACOS
WITH PICKLED RADISH

PREP + COOK TIME **45 MINUTES (+ STANDING)** SERVES **4**

2 CUPS (160G) SHREDDED WHITE CABBAGE

½ CUP COARSELY CHOPPED FRESH CORIANDER (CILANTRO)

¼ CUP (60ML) LIME JUICE

¼ CUP (60ML) OLIVE OIL

1 CUP (240G) SOUR CREAM

1 TABLESPOON SRIRACHA

400G (12½ OUNCES) SASHIMI-GRADE KINGFISH, CUT INTO 1.5CM (¾-INCH) PIECES

2 GREEN ONIONS (SCALLIONS), SLICED THINLY

8 X 7CM (2¾-INCH) WHITE CORN TORTILLAS

2 MEDIUM AVOCADOS (500G), CHOPPED COARSELY

2 TABLESPOONS FRESH OREGANO LEAVES

PICKLED RADISH

1 TEASPOON CUMIN SEEDS

¼ CUP (60ML) APPLE CIDER VINEGAR

1 TEASPOON CASTER SUGAR (SUPERFINE SUGAR)

PINCH SEA SALT FLAKES

6 RADISHES (210G), TRIMMED, SLICED THINLY

1 Make pickled radish.

2 Meanwhile, combine cabbage, coriander, 1 tablespoon of the juice and 1 tablespoon of the oil in a medium bowl; season to taste.

3 Combine sour cream and sauce in a small bowl; season to taste.

4 Combine fish, green onion, remaining juice and 1 tablespoon of the oil in a large glass bowl. Cover; refrigerate for 25 minutes or until fish is opaque and cooked (cured).

5 Meanwhile, cook tortillas on a lightly oiled heated grill plate (or grill) for 30 seconds each side or until golden and warmed through.

6 Serve tortillas topped with cabbage salad, fish, avocado, pickled radish, sour cream mixture and oregano; drizzle with remaining oil.

pickled radish Stir cumin seeds in a dry frying pan over medium heat for 2 minutes or until toasted and fragrant. Place seeds in a medium bowl with vinegar, sugar and salt; stir until sugar dissolves. Add radish; stand for 10 minutes.

nutritional count per serving
59.8g total fat (23g saturated fat); 3110kJ (744 cal); 21.3g carbohydrate; 27.3g protein; 6.8g fibre

tips Ceviche is a popular South American seafood dish that 'cooks' by marinating in citrus juice. Sriracha is a medium-hot chilli sauce available from Asian food stores and some major supermarkets.

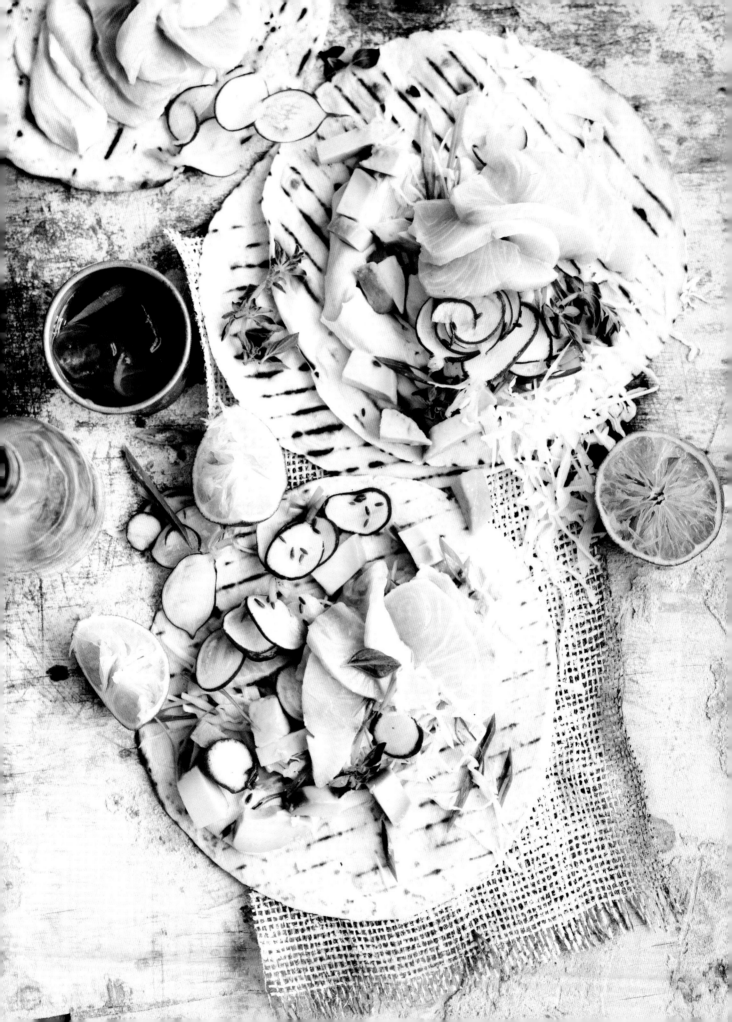

POTATO & SPINACH
FRITTATA

PREP + COOK TIME **40 MINUTES** SERVES **4**

500G (1 POUND) BABY NEW POTATOES
8 FREE-RANGE EGGS
⅔ CUP (160ML) MILK
1 TABLESPOON OLIVE OIL
100G (3 OUNCES) BABY SPINACH LEAVES
1 CUP (240G) CHARGRILLED RED CAPSICUM, DRAINED, CHOPPED COARSELY
100G (3 OUNCES) SOFT GOAT'S CHEESE, CRUMBLED
1 TABLESPOON LEMON RIND STRIPS (SEE TIP)

OLIVE SALSA
¼ CUP (55G) PITTED KALAMATA OLIVES, CHOPPED
¼ CUP (40G) PITTED GREEN SICILIAN OLIVES, CHOPPED
¼ CUP (40G) PITTED GREEN OLIVES, CHOPPED
½ SMALL RED ONION (50G), CHOPPED FINELY
¼ CUP CHOPPED FRESH FLAT-LEAF PARSLEY
PINCH DRIED CHILLI FLAKES
1 TABLESPOON OLIVE OIL
2 TEASPOONS LEMON JUICE

1 Place potatoes in a medium saucepan with enough cold water to just cover. Boil over medium heat for 15 minutes or until potato is tender; drain. Cut into 2.5cm (1-inch) pieces.
2 Meanwhile, make olive salsa.
3 Whisk eggs and milk in a medium bowl; season.
4 Preheat grill (broiler).
5 Heat oil in a heavy-based frying pan over medium-high heat; cook spinach until wilted. Add potatoes and capsicum; cook, stirring, for 1 minute. Add egg mixture. Reduce heat to medium; cook for 7 minutes or until egg is almost set. Top with cheese. Place under heated grill for 3 minutes or until golden and set.
6 Serve frittata with salsa; sprinkle with lemon rind.

olive salsa Combine ingredients in a small bowl.

nutritional count per serving
27.2g total fat (9.3g saturated fat); 1977kJ (473 cal); 30g carbohydrate; 24.7g protein; 5.5g fibre

tip If you have one, use a zester to create the strips of lemon rind. If you don't have one, peel two long, wide strips of rind from the lemon, without the white pith, then cut them lengthways into thin strips.

PEA & PRAWN
PATTIES

PREP + COOK TIME **45 MINUTES (+ REFRIGERATION)** SERVES **4**

1½ CUPS (180G) FROZEN PEAS
1 CLOVE GARLIC, PEELED
250G (4 OUNCES) PEELED
** UNCOOKED MEDIUM KING**
** PRAWNS (SHRIMP), CHOPPED**
1 TABLESPOON FRESH TARRAGON
** LEAVES, CHOPPED COARSELY**
½ TEASPOON FINELY GRATED
** LEMON RIND**
1 TABLESPOON GROUND
** ALMONDS**
2 CUPS (235G) FIRMLY PACKED
** TRIMMED WATERCRESS**
1 MEDIUM FENNEL BULB (300G),
** SLICED THINLY**
1 STALK CELERY (150G),
** TRIMMED, SLICED THINLY**
** ON THE DIAGONAL**
¼ CUP (40G) ROASTED WHOLE
** BLANCHED ALMONDS,**
** CHOPPED COARSELY**
1 TABLESPOON FRESH TARRAGON
** LEAVES, EXTRA**
2 TABLESPOONS DILL SPRIGS
2 TABLESPOONS OLIVE OIL
MUSTARD & LEMON DRESSING
1½ TABLESPOONS DIJON
** MUSTARD**
1 TABLESPOON LEMON JUICE
2 TABLESPOONS OLIVE OIL

1 Boil, steam or microwave peas and garlic together until peas are tender; drain.

2 Blend or process garlic and 1 cup of the peas with prawns, chopped tarragon, rind and ground almonds until combined; season. Using oiled hands, roll level tablespoons of mixture into 16 balls; flatten slightly. Cover; refrigerate for 1 hour. (The patties are quite sticky, however they will not fall apart during cooking.)

3 Meanwhile, make mustard and lemon dressing.

4 Place watercress, fennel, celery, blanched almonds, extra tarragon, dill and remaining peas in a large bowl with half the dressing; toss gently to combine.

5 Heat oil in a large non-stick frying pan over medium heat; cook patties, in batches, for 2 minutes each side or until golden and cooked through. Remove from pan; cover to keep warm.

6 Serve patties with watercress salad, drizzled with remaining dressing.

mustard & lemon dressing Whisk ingredients in a small bowl until combined; season to taste.

nutritional count per serving
25.4g total fat (3.5g saturated fat); 1507kJ (360 cal); 10g carbohydrate; 20.9g protein; 6.7g fibre

tips Use a mandoline or V-slicer to cut the fennel into very thin slices. Patties can be made up to 1 day ahead; store in an airtight container in the fridge.

MEDITATION IS NOT A LUXURY, IT'S A WAY TO DISCONNECT FROM OUR BUSY LIVES AND RECHARGE FOR THE NEXT CHALLENGE.

KUMARA, PROSCIUTTO
& MOZZARELLA
FLATBREADS

PREP + COOK TIME **45 MINUTES** SERVES **4**

400G (12½ OUNCES) KUMARA (ORANGE SWEET POTATO), SLICED THINLY

8 CHIA MOUNTAIN BREAD WRAPS (200G)

1 CUP (80G) FINELY GRATED PARMESAN

8 SLICES PROSCIUTTO (120G), TORN

¼ CUP FRESH SAGE LEAVES

2 TEASPOONS FINELY GRATED LEMON RIND

250G (8 OUNCES) SMOKED MOZZARELLA, SLICED THINLY

4 LARGE FRESH FIGS (320G), QUARTERED

70G (2½ OUNCES) BABY ROCKET (ARUGULA) LEAVES

1½ TABLESPOONS BALSAMIC VINEGAR

1 TABLESPOON OLIVE OIL

1 Preheat oven to 220°C/425°F. Line four oven trays with baking paper.

2 Cook kumara in boiling water for 5 minutes or until tender; drain.

3 Place four wraps on trays; sprinkle with parmesan. Top with remaining wraps, then kumara, prosciutto, sage, rind and mozzarella. Bake, in two batches, for 12 minutes or until golden and crisp.

4 Combine rocket, vinegar and oil in a large bowl. Divide figs and rocket mixture between flatbreads.

nutritional count per serving
30.9g total fat (15.7g saturated fat); 2629kJ (629 cal); 44.7g carbohydrate; 40g protein; 6.4g fibre

PEA, FENNEL & SPINACH
LASAGNE

PREP + COOK TIME **1 HOUR 10 MINUTES (+ COOLING)** SERVES **6**

¼ CUP (60ML) EXTRA VIRGIN
   OLIVE OIL
1 MEDIUM BULB FENNEL (300G),
   CHOPPED FINELY
2 CLOVES GARLIC, CRUSHED
2 SHALLOTS (50G),
   CHOPPED FINELY
1 TEASPOON GROUND FENNEL
2 TEASPOONS FINELY GRATED
   LEMON RIND
500G (1 POUND) SPINACH,
   TRIMMED
1½ CUPS (240G) FRESH PEAS
1.2KG (2½ POUNDS) CANNED
   CHOPPED TOMATOES
1 CUP ROUGHLY TORN FRESH
   BASIL LEAVES
250G (8 OUNCES) WHOLEMEAL
   LASAGNE SHEETS
¼ CUP (60G) SOFT RICOTTA
2 TABLESPOONS EXTRA VIRGIN
   OLIVE OIL, EXTRA
¼ CUP SMALL BASIL LEAVES,
   EXTRA
RICOTTA BCHAMEL
1¾ CUPS (420G) SOFT RICOTTA
3 FREE-RANGE EGGS
½ CUP (140G) GREEK-STYLE
   YOGHURT
¼ CUP (60ML) LEMON JUICE
1 CUP (200G) CRUMBLED FETTA
½ CUP (125ML) SPARKLING
   MINERAL WATER

1 Heat 1½ tablespoons of the oil in a large frying pan over medium heat; cook chopped fennel, garlic, shallots and ground fennel, stirring, for 8 minutes or until lightly golden. Transfer mixture to a large bowl; stir in rind. Season to taste.

2 Wash spinach leaves but don't dry. Cook spinach in same pan over high heat, in two batches, until wilted; drain. When cool enough to handle, squeeze out excess liquid. Coarsely chop spinach; stir into fennel mixture. Season to taste. Refrigerate until cooled. Stir in peas.

3 Preheat oven to 200°C/400°F.

4 Combine tomatoes, basil and remaining oil in a bowl; season.

5 Make ricotta béchamel.

6 Spread one-third of the tomato mixture over the base of a 3 litre (12-cup) baking dish. Cover with one-third of the pasta sheets. Top with half the spinach mixture and half the ricotta béchamel. Continue layering with remaining pasta sheets, tomato mixture, spinach mixture and ricotta béchamel, finishing with pasta sheets and tomato mixture. Top with spoonfuls of ricotta.

7 Bake lasagne for 45 minutes or until top is golden and pasta is cooked (cover with greased foil if necessary to prevent overbrowning). Stand for 10 minutes before serving. Serve lasagne drizzled with extra oil and topped with extra basil.

ricotta béchamel Whisk ricotta, eggs, yoghurt, juice and fetta in a large bowl until combined. Whisk mineral water into mixture until combined.

nutritional count per serving
35g total fat (13.5g saturated fat); 2637kJ (630 cal); 43.6g carbohydrate; 29.3g protein; 11.8g fibre

STIR-FRIED PUMPKIN
& WATER SPINACH

PREP + COOK TIME **15 MINUTES** SERVES **4**

¼ CUP (60G) EXTRA VIRGIN COCONUT OIL, MELTED

650G (1¼ POUNDS) JAP PUMPKIN, PEELED, CUT INTO 3CM (1¼-INCH) PIECES

2 TEASPOONS CHINESE FIVE-SPICE POWDER

¼ CUP (60ML) MUSHROOM OYSTER-FLAVOURED SAUCE

¼ CUP (60ML) WATER

6CM (2½-INCH) PIECE FRESH GINGER (30G), CUT INTO FINE MATCHSTICKS

185G (6 OUNCES) WATER SPINACH, TRIMMED, CUT INTO THIRDS

250G (8 OUNCES) CHERRY TOMATOES, HALVED

¹/₃ CUP (20G) FLAKED ALMONDS, TOASTED

1 Heat 2 tablespoons of the coconut oil in a large wok over medium heat; cook pumpkin pieces, turning frequently, for 6 minutes until almost tender. Remove from wok.

2 Meanwhile, combine five-spice, sauce and the water in a small bowl.

3 Heat remaining oil in wok over medium-high heat; stir-fry ginger for 1 minute or until crisp. Add water spinach, tomatoes and five-spice mixture; stir-fry for 1 minute or until water spinach wilts. Return pumpkin to wok; stir through.

4 Serve stir-fry topped with almonds.

nutritional count per serving
18.5g total fat (14g saturated fat); 1119kJ (267 cal); 17.6g carbohydrate; 4.6g protein; 6.5g fibre

tips Coconut oil is a solidified oil sold in jars and is available from major supermarkets and health food stores. Melt coconut oil as you would butter, either in a small saucepan over low heat or in the microwave. You will need about 1 bunch of water spinach for this recipe.

BUCKWHEAT SOBA NOODLES
& MISO SALMON

PREP + COOK TIME **30 MINUTES (+ COOLING)** SERVES **4**

270G (8½ OUNCES) BUCKWHEAT SOBA NOODLES

1 TABLESPOON MISO PASTE (LIGHT)

1 TABLESPOON RICE WINE VINEGAR

1 TABLESPOON RICE MALT SYRUP

1 TABLESPOON VEGETABLE OIL

2 X 280G (9-OUNCE) SALMON FILLETS, SKIN REMOVED

8 GREEN ONIONS (SCALLIONS), TRIMMED, HALVED

150G (4½ OUNCES) SNOW PEAS

1 TABLESPOON FINELY GRATED FRESH GINGER

¼ CUP (60ML) SOY SAUCE

2 TABLESPOONS MIRIN

1 TEASPOON SESAME OIL

1 GREEN ONION (SCALLION), EXTRA, SLICED THINLY

2 TEASPOONS BLACK SESAME SEEDS

1 Preheat oven to 200°C/400°F.

2 Cook noodles in a large saucepan of boiling salted water for 3 minutes or until just tender. Drain; keep warm.

3 Combine miso, vinegar, syrup and half the vegetable oil in a large bowl. Add salmon; toss to coat. Arrange green onion, side-by-side, on an oven tray; place salmon on top. Drizzle with remaining vegetable oil. Roast for 10 minutes or until salmon is cooked as desired.

4 Meanwhile, boil, steam or microwave snow peas until just tender; drain. Refresh in a bowl of iced water; drain.

5 Place noodles in a medium bowl with ginger, soy sauce, mirin and sesame oil; toss to coat. Flake salmon onto noodles, add cooked green onion and snow peas; toss gently to combine. Serve topped with extra green onion and the sesame seeds.

nutritional count per serving

18.2g total fat (3.1g saturated fat); 2443kJ (583 cal); 64g carbohydrate; 39g protein; 3.4g fibre

tip Salmon can be refrigerated in the marinade up to 3 hours before cooking.

MUSSEL & CHICKPEA
KORMA

PREP + COOK TIME **35 MINUTES** SERVES **4**

2 TABLESPOONS OLIVE OIL

1 MEDIUM LEEK (350G), WHITE
   PART ONLY, SLICED

2 CLOVES GARLIC, CRUSHED

⅓ CUP (100G) KORMA PASTE

300G (9½ OUNCES) KUMARA
   (ORANGE SWEET POTATO),
   DICED

270ML COCONUT MILK

1 CUP (250ML) FISH STOCK

400G (12½ OUNCES) CANNED
   DICED TOMATOES

800G (1½ POUNDS) CANNED
   CHICKPEAS (GARBANZO
   BEANS), DRAINED, RINSED

1KG (2 POUNDS) BLACK MUSSELS,
   SCRUBBED, BEARDED

250G (8 OUNCES) BABY SPINACH

½ CUP FRESH CORIANDER
   (CILANTRO) LEAVES

1 Heat oil in a large saucepan over medium-high heat; cook leek and garlic, stirring for 2 minutes or until softened.

2 Add korma paste to pan; cook, stirring, for 2 minutes. Add kumara, coconut milk, stock, tomatoes and chickpeas; bring to the boil. Reduce heat; simmer for 6 minutes or until kumara is tender. Stir in mussels; cook, covered, for 4 minutes or until mussels open. Stir in spinach until wilted. Serve topped with coriander.

nutritional count per serving

36.6g total fat (15.4g saturated fat); 2606kJ (623 cal); 41.9g carbohydrate; 25.5g protein; 12.8g fibre

serving suggestion Serve with steamed basmati rice.

ROAST CHICKEN
WITH BROAD BEANS

PREP + COOK TIME **1 HOUR 15 MINUTES** SERVES **4**

If you prefer, you can use a 1.5kg (3-pound) whole chicken chopped into pieces instead of buying chicken pieces.

1 MEDIUM LEMON (140G)

3 CUPS (375G) FRESH SHELLED BROAD (FAVA) BEANS

2 TABLESPOONS OLIVE OIL

1.5KG (3 POUNDS) CHICKEN PIECES, BONE-IN, SKIN-ON

4 GREEN ONIONS (SCALLIONS), CUT INTO 4CM (1½-INCH) LENGTHS

4 CLOVES GARLIC, SLICED THINLY

8 SPRIGS FRESH THYME

1½ CUPS (375ML) CHICKEN STOCK

2 TABLESPOONS LEMON JUICE

½ CUP LOOSELY PACKED FRESH MINT LEAVES

2 TABLESPOONS CAPERS, RINSED

1 Preheat oven to 200°C/400°F.

2 Using a vegetable peeler, peel four 7cm (2¾-inch) strips of rind from the lemon. Squeeze juice from the lemon; you need 2 tablespoons juice.

3 Cook broad beans in a saucepan of boiling water 2 minutes; drain. Refresh under cold running water; drain. Peel away skins then discard.

4 Heat oil in a large casserole dish over high heat; cook chicken pieces, in two batches, for 3 minutes each side or until browned. Remove from dish; drain excess fat from dish.

5 Add onion, garlic, thyme and rind strips to same dish; cook for 2 minutes. Return chicken and any juices to the dish with stock; bring to the boil. Transfer to the oven; cook, uncovered, for 40 minutes or until chicken is cooked through. Stir in broad beans; cook for a further 5 minutes or until heated through.

6 Serve chicken drizzled with lemon juice, topped with mint and capers.

nutritional count per serving

32.5g total fat (8.5g saturated fat); 2181kJ (521 cal); 5.9g carbohydrate; 47.3g protein; 9g fibre

tips You will need to buy about 1.7kg (3½ pounds) fresh broad beans in the pod to yield 3 cups, or you can use frozen broad beans. You can cook baby potatoes with the chicken.

serving suggestion Serve with wholemeal couscous.

STEAK WITH CASHEW
NAM JIM

PREP + COOK TIME **40 MINUTES** SERVES **4**

800G (1½ POUNDS) THICK-CUT BEEF RUMP STEAK

1 TABLESPOON OLIVE OIL

350G (11 OUNCES) GAI LAN

270G (8½ OUNCES) BABY BUK CHOY, TRIMMED, QUARTERED

100G (3 OUNCES) SNOW PEAS

4 GREEN ONIONS (SCALLIONS), SLICED THINLY

¼ CUP (40G) UNSALTED ROASTED CASHEWS, CHOPPED

¼ CUP LOOSELY PACKED FRESH CORIANDER (CILANTRO) SPRIGS

CASHEW NAM JIM

2 SHALLOTS (50G), CHOPPED

2 CLOVES GARLIC

3 FRESH LONG GREEN CHILLIES, SEEDED, CHOPPED COARSELY

2 FRESH CORIANDER (CILANTRO) ROOTS, CHOPPED COARSELY

½ TEASPOON FINELY GRATED FRESH GINGER

2 TABLESPOONS GRATED DARK PALM SUGAR

⅓ CUP (50G) UNSALTED ROASTED CASHEWS

⅓ CUP (80ML) LIME JUICE, APPROXIMATELY

1 TABLESPOON FISH SAUCE, APPROXIMATELY

1 Make cashew nam jim.

2 Trim fat from steak; rub with oil, season. Cook steak on a heated grill plate (or grill or barbecue) on medium-high heat for 4 minutes each side for medium or until done as desired. Remove steak from heat; cover with foil, rest for 5 minutes.

3 Meanwhile, trim gai lan stalks; cut stalks from leaves. Steam stalks, in a single layer, in a large steamer over a wok or large saucepan of boiling water for 1 minute. Place buk choy on top of gai lan; steam for a further 2 minutes. Add snow peas and gai lan leaves; steam for a further 2 minutes or until vegetables are just tender.

4 Place vegetables on a platter in layers, top with thickly sliced steak; drizzle with any steak juices, then top with cashew nam jim. Sprinkle with onion, nuts and coriander.

cashew nam jim Blend shallots, garlic, chilli, coriander root, ginger, sugar and nuts (or pound with a mortar and pestle) until mixture forms a paste. Transfer to a small bowl; stir in juice and fish sauce to taste.

nutritional count per serving

35g total fat (9.7g saturated fat); 2888kJ (670 cal); 14g carbohydrate; 76.4g protein; 7.4g fibre

tips You will need about 3 limes for this recipe. Nam jim can be made a day ahead; keep tightly covered in the fridge until ready to use.

serving suggestion Serve with steamed jasmine or brown rice.

SPANISH
PORK CUTLETS

PREP + COOK TIME **1 HOUR** SERVES **2**

1 BUNCH BABY (DUTCH) CARROTS, TRIMMED, PEELED
1 MEDIUM RED CAPSICUM (BELL PEPPER) (200G), CHOPPED COARSELY
200G (6½ OUNCES) BRUSSELS SPROUTS, HALVED
1 LARGE RED ONION (300G), CUT INTO WEDGES
3 CLOVES GARLIC, UNPEELED
1 TEASPOON SMOKED PAPRIKA
2 TEASPOONS OLIVE OIL
1 MEDIUM TOMATO (150G), QUARTERED
2 PORK CUTLETS (470G), TRIMMED
200G (6½ OUNCES) GREEN BEANS, TRIMMED
1 TABLESPOON ROASTED ALMOND KERNELS

1 Preheat oven to 220°C/425°F.
2 Place carrots, capsicum, sprouts, onion and garlic in a large baking dish. Sprinkle with paprika, drizzle with half the oil; toss vegetables to coat. Bake for 40 minutes or until vegetables are golden and tender; add tomato to dish 10 minutes before end of cooking time.
3 Meanwhile, brush pork with remaining oil; cook pork on a heated grill plate (or grill or barbecue) for 4 minutes each side or until cooked as you like. Remove from heat; cover, rest for 5 minutes.
4 Boil, steam or microwave beans until tender; cover to keep warm.
5 Squeeze garlic from skin. Blend or process garlic, tomato, nuts and half the capsicum until mixture is smooth.
6 Divide pork, roasted vegetables and beans between serving plates; serve topped with tomato and almond sauce.

nutritional count per serving
11.9g total fat (1.9g saturated fat); 1836kJ (439 cal); 25.3g carbohydrate; 46.4g protein 21.2g fibre

tips You can use any colour baby carrots; purple, yellow or white, or a mixture of colours. The sauce would also go well with roasted chicken.

LAMB KOFTAS WITH
WHITE BEANS

PREP + COOK TIME **40 MINUTES (+ COOLING)** SERVES **4**

400G (12½ OUNCES) CANNED WHITE BEANS, DRAINED, RINSED

1 TABLESPOON LEMON JUICE

2 TABLESPOONS FRESH OREGANO LEAVES

2 TABLESPOONS OLIVE OIL

½ CUP (35G) FRESH BREADCRUMBS

2 TABLESPOON MILK

600G (1¼ POUNDS) MINCED (GROUND) LAMB

1 TEASPOON GROUND ALLSPICE

⅓ CUP FRESH OREGANO LEAVES, EXTRA, CHOPPED

100G (3 OUNCES) FETTA, CRUMBLED

1 BABY COS (ROMAINE) LETTUCE, TRIMMED, LEAVES SEPARATED

BEETROOT TZATZIKI

200G (6½ OUNCES) BEETROOT (BEETS), PEELED, GRATED

1 CUP (280G) GREEK-STYLE YOGHURT

2 TABLESPOONS CHOPPED FRESH MINT

1 CLOVE GARLIC, CRUSHED

1 TABLESPOON FINELY GRATED LEMON RIND

1 Make beetroot tzatiki.

2 Combine white beans, juice, oregano and half the oil in a medium bowl. Season to taste.

3 Place breadcrumbs and milk in a medium bowl; stand for 3 minutes or until milk has been absorbed. Add lamb, allspice and extra oregano; season. Using your hands, work mixture until well combined. Add fetta; stir until combined. Roll heaped tablespoonful measures of lamb mixture into kofta shapes.

4 Heat remaining oil in a large non-stick frying pan over medium-high heat; cook kofta, turning occasionally, for 10 minutes or until browned and cooked through.

5 Serve kofta on lettuce with bean mixture and tzatziki.

beetroot tzatziki Combine ingredients in a medium bowl; season to taste.

nutritional count per serving
41g total fat (16.4g saturated fat); 2680kJ (640 cal); 21.4g carbohydrate; 44.5g protein; 4.9g fibre

tip Cooked or uncooked kofta can be frozen for up to 3 months. Thaw in the fridge before reheating or cooking.

CHILLI LIME SNAPPER
WITH CORN SALSA SALAD

PREP + COOK TIME **35 MINUTES** SERVES **4**

¼ CUP (60ML) OLIVE OIL

1 CLOVE GARLIC, SLICED THINLY

1 FRESH LONG GREEN CHILLI, SEEDED, CHOPPED FINELY

1 TEASPOON FINELY GRATED LIME RIND

4 X 180G (5½-OUNCE) BONELESS, SKINLESS SNAPPER FILLETS

2 CORN COBS (250G), HUSKS REMOVED

6 RED RADISHES (90G), SLICED THINLY

45G (1½ OUNCES) SNOW PEA SPROUTS, TRIMMED

1 GREEN ONION (SCALLION), SLICED THINLY

¼ CUP LOOSELY PACKED FRESH CORIANDER (CILANTRO) LEAVES

1 TABLESPOON LIME JUICE

1 TABLESPOON WHITE BALSAMIC VINEGAR OR WHITE VINEGAR

1 TABLESPOON OLIVE OIL, EXTRA

1 MEDIUM AVOCADO (250G), SLICED

LIME WEDGES, TO SERVE

1 Combine 2 tablespoons of the oil with garlic, chilli and rind in a small bowl; add snapper, turn to coat. Set aside.

2 Brush corn with remaining oil; cook on a heated chargrill plate (or barbecue), turning every 2 minutes, for 8 minutes or until corn is cooked and lightly charred. Cool.

3 Place radish, sprouts, green onion and coriander in a bowl of iced water to crisp.

4 Cut kernels from cooled cobs; place in a large bowl with juice, vinegar and extra oil. Remove radish mixture from water with a slotted spoon; drain on paper towel. Add to corn mixture, season to taste; toss gently to combine.

5 Line the chargrill plate with baking paper (ensure paper doesn't extend over the edge); cook snapper on heated plate, for 2 minutes each side or until just cooked through.

6 Serve snapper with corn salsa salad, avocado and lime.

nutritional count per serving

32.3g total fat (6g saturated fat); 2465kJ (589 cal); 25.5g carbohydrate; 44.5g protein; 8.9g fibre

tip You can use any firm white fish fillets you prefer or prawns for this recipe.

QUINOA & CAULIFLOWER
'COUSCOUS'

PREP + COOK TIME **45 MINUTES** SERVES **4**

¾ CUP (150G) RED QUINOA, RINSED WELL

1½ CUPS (375ML) WATER

1 MEDIUM CAULIFLOWER (1.25KG), TRIMMED

1 TABLESPOON EXTRA VIRGIN OLIVE OIL

1 LARGE BROWN ONION (200G), CHOPPED FINELY

2 TEASPOONS GROUND CUMIN

½ CUP (80G) COARSELY CHOPPED ROASTED PISTACHIOS

1 TABLESPOON DRIED CURRANTS

2 TEASPOONS FINELY CHOPPED PRESERVED LEMON RIND

¼ CUP (60ML) LEMON JUICE

¼ CUP (60ML) EXTRA VIRGIN OLIVE OIL, EXTRA

1 CUP COARSELY CHOPPED FRESH FLAT-LEAF PARSLEY

150G (4½ OUNCES) FETTA, CRUMBLED

1 SMALL POMEGRANATE (250G), SEEDS REMOVED (SEE TIP)

1 Place quinoa in a medium saucepan with the water; bring to the boil. Reduce heat to low; cook, covered, for 12 minutes or until the water is absorbed and quinoa is tender. Season to taste.

2 Meanwhile, cut cauliflower into florets; process, in batches, until very finely chopped.

3 Heat oil in a medium frying pan over high heat. Add onion, reduce heat to low; cook, stirring occasionally, for 10 minutes or until caramelised. Stir in cumin, then add cauliflower. Increase heat to medium; cook, stirring occasionally, for 6 minutes or until cauliflower is tender. Season to taste.

4 Add quinoa to pan with remaining ingredients; stir to combine. Season to taste.

nutritional count per serving
40.3g total fat (10g saturated fat); 2722kJ (651 cal); 39.5g carbohydrate; 23.9g protein; 16.4g fibre

tip To remove pomegranate seeds, cut a pomegranate in half crossways; hold it, cut-side down, in the palm of your hand over a bowl, then hit the outside firmly with a wooden spoon. The seeds should fall out easily; discard any white pith that falls out with them. Pomegranate seeds will keep in the fridge for up to a week. Fresh pomegranate seeds can sometimes be found in the fridge section of supermarkets and good greengrocers; you will need ½ cup (75g) for this recipe.

BODY SCRUBS

CITRUS SALT SCRUB *Combine 1 cup organic sea salt, ¼ cup sweet almond oil, ½ teaspoon grated lemon rind and ½ teaspoon grated orange rind. Store in an airtight container in a cool, dry place. Stir before use. This invigorating scrub is great for glowing skin.*

COFFEE BODY SCRUB

Combine ¼ cup ground coffee, ¼ cup raw sugar, ¼ cup coconut oil and 1 tablespoon sea salt flakes in a medium bowl. Gently scrub, in a light, circular motion, all over the body. Wash off in warm water. This scrub invigorates and wakes up the skin, and helps to battle cellulite.

Green tea SUGAR SCRUB

Combine 1½ cups white sugar, the leaves from 2 green tea bags and 2 teaspoons green tea powder until mixed well. Stir in 1 cup melted coconut oil. This scrub is a natural remedy for fighting cellulite and removing toxins.

LEMON & ROSEMARY SCRUB

Combine ½ cup white sugar, ½ cup extra virgin olive oil, 2 teaspoons finely grated lemon rind, 2 tablespoons lemon juice, 2 teaspoons rosemary essential oil, 1 tablespoon bicarbonate of soda. Gently scrub, in a light, circular motion, all over the body. Wash off in warm water. As well as smelling great, this scrub is high in antioxidants and helps to even out pigmentation, reduce fine lines and stimulates skin growth and repair.

PRAWN BARLEY RISOTTO
WITH CHILLI GREMOLATA

PREP + COOK TIME **50 MINUTES** SERVES **4**

1 TABLESPOON OLIVE OIL

1 MEDIUM BROWN ONION (150G), CHOPPED FINELY

2 CLOVES GARLIC, CRUSHED

1½ CUPS (300G) PEARL BARLEY

1 LITRE (4 CUPS) VEGETABLE STOCK OR WATER

500G (1 POUND) PEELED UNCOOKED MEDIUM KING PRAWNS (SHRIMP)

45G (1½ OUNCES) BABY ROCKET (ARUGULA) LEAVES

¼ CUP (20G) FINELY GRATED PARMESAN

160G (5 OUNCES) LABNE (SEE TIPS)

CHILLI GREMOLATA

1 TABLESPOON FINELY GRATED LEMON RIND (SEE TIPS)

1 FRESH LONG RED CHILLI, SEEDED, CHOPPED FINELY

2 TABLESPOONS FINELY CHOPPED FRESH FLAT-LEAF PARSLEY

1 Heat oil in a large saucepan over medium-high heat; cook onion and garlic, stirring, for 5 minutes or until onion softens. Add barley; cook, stirring, for 1 minute or until coated. Add stock; bring to the boil. Reduce heat to low; simmer, covered, for 30 minutes or until barley is almost tender.

2 Add prawns; simmer, uncovered, for 5 minutes or until barley is tender and liquid is absorbed. Add parmesan and rocket; stir to combine.

3 Make chilli gremolata.

4 Serve risotto topped with labne and chilli gremolata.

chilli gremolata Combine ingredients in a small bowl.

nutritional count per serving
13g total fat (4.2g saturated fat); 2090kJ (500 cal); 52.5g carbohydrate; 38.7g protein; 10.3g fibre

tips Labne is a soft fresh cheese made from strained yoghurt, generally it is rolled into balls and stored in olive oil. If you have one, use a zester to create strips of lemon rind instead of grating the rind. If you don't have one, peel two long, wide strips of rind from the lemon, without the white pith, then cut them lengthways into thin strips.

CORN & BLACK BEAN
ENCHILADAS

PREP + COOK TIME **1 HOUR 40 MINUTES** SERVES **4**

3 LARGE ZUCCHINI (450G)

⅓ CUP (80ML) OLIVE OIL

2 TRIMMED CORN COBS (500G)

8 X 20CM (8-INCH) WHITE CORN TORTILLAS

400G (12½ OUNCES) CANNED BLACK BEANS, DRAINED, RINSED

½ CUP FRESH CORIANDER (CILANTRO) LEAVES

100G (3 OUNCES) FETTA

¼ CUP FRESH OREGANO LEAVES

1 TABLESPOON FRESH OREGANO, EXTRA

ENCHILADA SAUCE

800G (1½ POUNDS) CANNED CRUSHED TOMATOES

1½ CUPS (375ML) VEGETABLE STOCK

2 TABLESPOONS OLIVE OIL

2 TABLESPOON COARSELY CHOPPED FRESH OREGANO

2 TABLESPOON APPLE CIDER VINEGAR

1 MEDIUM BROWN ONION (150G), CHOPPED COARSELY

1 CLOVE GARLIC, CHOPPED

1 TABLESPOON CHOPPED PICKLED JALAPEÑOS

1 TEASPOON GROUND CUMIN

1 TEASPOON CASTER SUGAR (SUPERFINE SUGAR)

¼ TEASPOON GROUND CHILLI POWDER

1 Preheat oven to 180°C/350°F. Line an oven tray with baking paper. Grease a 25cm x 30cm (10-inch x 12-inch) ovenproof dish.

2 Cut zucchini in half lengthways, then each half into long thin wedges. Place zucchini on tray; drizzle with half the oil. Roast for 30 minutes or until just tender; chop coarsely.

3 Meanwhile make enchilada sauce.

4 Brush corn with 1 tablespoon of the oil. Heat a grill plate (or grill or barbecue) over medium-high heat; cook corn, turning occasionally, for 10 minutes or until golden and tender. Using a sharp knife, cut kernels from cobs; discard cobs.

5 Reheat grill plate (or grill or barbecue) over medium-high heat; cook tortillas, for 30 seconds each side or until lightly charred. Transfer to a plate; cover to keep warm.

6 Combine zucchini, beans, coriander, half the corn, half the fetta, half the oregano and ½ cup enchilada sauce in a large bowl.

7 Divide zucchini filling evenly among warm tortillas; roll to enclose filling. Place tortillas in dish; brush tops with remaining oil. Spoon remaining enchilada sauce over tortillas, leaving 2cm (¾-inch) at each end of enchiladas uncovered. Top with remaining fetta and oregano.

8 Bake enchiladas for 30 minutes or until golden and heated through. Serve topped with remaining corn and extra oregano.

enchilada sauce Blend or process ingredients until smooth; transfer to a medium saucepan. Bring to a simmer. Simmer over medium heat for 20 minutes or until sauce is thickened slightly.

nutritional count per serving
35.5g total fat (8.5g saturated fat); 2320kJ (555 cal); 36.1g carbohydrate; 16.3g protein; 13.3g fibre

CHICKEN & ZUCCHINI WITH
SALSA VERDE

PREP + COOK TIME **30 MINUTES** SERVES **4**

4 CHICKEN BREAST FILLETS (680G), HALVED LENGTHWAYS
1 TABLESPOON OLIVE OIL
5 MEDIUM ZUCCHINI (500G)
⅓ CUP (25G) FLAKED ALMONDS, TOASTED
100G (3 OUNCES) GOAT'S FETTA, CRUMBLED
¼ CUP FRESH FLAT-LEAF PARSLEY LEAVES

SALSA VERDE
½ CUP COARSELY CHOPPED FRESH FLAT-LEAF PARSLEY
¼ CUP COARSELY CHOPPED FRESH BASIL
1 CLOVE GARLIC, CRUSHED
2 TEASPOONS DRAINED BABY CAPERS, RINSED
1 TEASPOON DIJON MUSTARD
¼ CUP (60ML) OLIVE OIL
2 TEASPOONS RED WINE VINEGAR

1 Season chicken with salt and pepper. Heat oil in a large frying pan over medium-high heat; cook chicken, in batches, for 4 minutes each side or until browned and cooked through. Remove from pan; cover to keep warm.

2 Using a spiralizer (see tip), cut zucchini into spirals.

3 Make salsa verde.

4 Serve chicken with zucchini topped with salsa verde, almonds, fetta and parsley.

salsa verde Combine parsley, basil, garlic and capers in a small bowl; whisk in mustard, oil and vinegar until thickened.

nutritional count per serving
31.8g total fat (8.6g saturated fat); 2030kJ (485 cal); 2.7g carbohydrate; 45.6g protein; 3.7g fibre

tip A spiralizer is a kitchen gadget that cuts vegetables into long thin spirals. If you don't have one, you can use a mandoline or V-slicer.

AFTERNOON

PICK ME UP

APPLE & PEPITA

PREP TIME **20 MINUTES** (+ REFRIGERATION)

MAKES **35**

Process 1 cup natural sliced almonds until finely chopped. Add 200g (6½oz) chopped medjool dates, 50g (1½oz) coarsely chopped dried apple, ¼ cup shredded coconut and ½ cup pepitas (pumpkin seeds); process until well combined. Add about 2 teaspoons hot water; process until mixture comes together. With damp hands, roll 2 level teaspoons of mixture into balls. Rolls balls in 1 cup shredded coconut to coat; place on a baking-paper-lined oven tray. Refrigerate for 1 hour.

MACADAMIA & FIG

PREP TIME **20 MINUTES** (+ REFRIGERATION)

MAKES **30**

Process 1 cup macadamias until finely chopped. Add 200g (6½oz) chopped medjool dates, 75g (2½oz) soft and juicy dried figs, 2 tablespoons white chia seeds and ½ teaspoon ground cinnamon; process until well combined. Add about 2 teaspoons hot water; process until mixture comes together. With damp hands, roll 2 level teaspoons of mixture into balls. Roll balls in 1 cup white chia seeds to coat; place on a baking-paper-lined oven tray. Refrigerate for 1 hour.

THESE WILL KEEP IN AN AIRTIGHT CONTAINER IN THE FRIDGE FOR UP TO 2 WEEKS.

BLISS BALLS

CRUNCHY MAC

FRUITY BURST

CACAO & HAZELNUT

PREP TIME 20 MINUTES (+ REFRIGERATION)

MAKES 30

Process 1 cup roasted skinless hazelnuts until finely chopped; reserve. Process another 1 cup roasted skinless hazelnuts until finely chopped. Add 200g (6½oz) chopped medjool dates, 2 tablespoons cacao powder and ½ teaspoon ground nutmeg; process until well combined. Add about 2 teaspoons hot water; process until mixture comes together. With damp hands, roll 2 level teaspoons of mixture into balls. Roll balls in reserved nuts to coat; place on a baking-paper-lined oven tray. Refrigerate for 1 hour.

PISTACHIO & CRANBERRY

PREP TIME 20 MINUTES (+ REFRIGERATION)

MAKES 35

Process 1 cup shelled pistachios until finely chopped; reserve. Process another 1 cup shelled pistachios until finely chopped. Add 200g (6½oz) chopped medjool dates and ½ cup dried unsweetened cranberries; process until well combined. Add about 2 teaspoons hot water; process until mixture comes together. With damp hands, roll 2 level teaspoons of mixture into balls. Roll balls in reserved nuts to coat; place on a baking-paper-lined oven tray. Refrigerate for 1 hour.

NUTTY CHOC

BERRY TANG

SALTED DATE
CARAMELS

PREP + COOK TIME **20 MINUTES (+ STANDING & FREEZING)** MAKES **16**

2 CUPS (310G) FRESH DATES, PITTED
¾ CUP (150G) VIRGIN COCONUT OIL
¼ CUP (25G) CACAO POWDER
1 TEASPOON VANILLA EXTRACT
2 TABLESPOONS VIRGIN COCONUT OIL, EXTRA, AT ROOM TEMPERATURE
½ TEASPOON SEA SALT FLAKES
¼ CUP (50G) COCONUT FLOUR
SEA SALT FLAKES, EXTRA

1 Place dates in a medium bowl, cover with boiling water; stand for 10 minutes to soften. Drain dates; discard water.

2 Meanwhile, melt oil in a small saucepan; combine oil and sifted cacao in a small bowl. Stand until thickened slightly.

3 Process dates, extract, extra oil and salt until smooth. Transfer mixture to a small bowl, cover; freeze for 30 minutes or until firm.

4 Line an oven tray with baking paper. Place coconut flour in a small bowl. Using damp hands, roll tablespoonfuls of the date mixture into balls. Roll balls in coconut flour. Using a spoon, dip date balls into cacao coating, then place on tray. Sprinkle with extra salt. Freeze for 10 minutes or until set.

nutritional count per ball
12.1g total fat (11.2g saturated fat); 657kJ (157 cal); 12.6g carbohydrate; 1.3g protein; 1.2g fibre

tips Don't worry if the coating on the caramels has a slight whitish look to it, this is simply the coconut fat, but it won't affect the taste. Store and eat the caramels straight from the freezer. Place the caramels in small paper cases to serve.

BROWN RICE
ENERGY BALLS

PREP + COOK TIME **1 HOUR (+ REFRIGERATION)** MAKES **12**

Turn this snack into lunch, by stuffing them into a pitta pocket or wrap with salad ingredients and a little dressing made from greek-style yoghurt, a couple of teaspoons of tahini and lemon juice.

1 CUP (200G) MEDIUM-GRAIN BROWN RICE
2½ CUPS (625ML) CHICKEN STOCK
2 TABLESPOONS TAHINI
1 TABLESPOON TAMARI
1 TABLESPOON APPLE CIDER VINEGAR
2 TABLESPOONS CHIA SEEDS
2 GREEN ONIONS (SCALLIONS), CHOPPED FINELY
2 TEASPOONS FINELY GRATED FRESH GINGER
2 TABLESPOONS BLACK SESAME SEEDS
2 TABLESPOONS WHITE SESAME SEEDS

1 Rinse rice under running water until water runs clear. Place rice in a medium saucepan with stock; bring to the boil. Reduce heat to low; cook, covered, for 40 minutes or until stock is almost absorbed and rice is tender. Remove from heat; stand, covered, for 5 minutes.

2 Transfer hot rice to a medium bowl; immediately stir in tahini, tamari, vinegar, chia seeds, green onion and ginger, season to taste. Stand for 5 minutes or until cool enough to handle.

3 Roll 2 tablespoons of mixture into balls; roll in combined sesame seeds. Place balls on a baking-paper-lined tray. Refrigerate at least 30 minutes before eating.

nutritional count per ball

6g total fat (0.7g saturated fat); 527kJ (126 cal); 13.4g carbohydrate; 3.7g protein; 2.1g fibre

tips As with meat, ingredients containing rice should always be kept refrigerated and never left at room temperature, otherwise food poisoning can occur. Rice balls will keep in the fridge for up to 5 days.

CHOCOLATE
HAZELNUT
SPREAD

PREP TIME **10 MINUTES**   MAKES **2 CUPS**

Use this homemade spread as a filling for cakes or cookies, or spread onto bread.

½ CUPS (210G) ROASTED
   SKINLESS HAZELNUTS (SEE TIP)
¼ CUP (25G) CACAO POWDER
¼ TEASPOON SEA SALT FLAKES
½ CUP (125ML) UNSWEETENED
   ALMOND MILK
⅓ CUP (80ML) PURE MAPLE
   SYRUP
1 TABLESPOON VANILLA
   EXTRACT
1 TABLESPOON VIRGIN
   COCONUT OIL

1 Place ingredients in a blender; blend for 5 minutes, scraping down the sides occasionally, until smooth.
2 Spoon spread into a small airtight container. Store in the fridge for up to 1 month.

nutritional count per tablespoon
30.7g total fat (5.7g saturated fat); 1545kJ (369 cal); 21.4g carbohydrate; 7.8g protein; 4.1g fibre

tip To roast and peel your own hazelnuts, spread nuts on an oven tray and roast at 180°C/350°F for 8 minutes or until golden. Rub warm hazelnuts in a clean tea towel to remove the skins. Cool.

ROASTED SESAME
EDAMAME BEANS

PREP + COOK TIME **25 MINUTES** SERVES **4**

500G (1 POUND) EDAMAME (SOY BEANS), SHELLED (SEE TIP)
2 TEASPOONS OLIVE OIL
2 TEASPOONS BLACK SESAME SEEDS
2 TEASPOONS WHITE SESAME SEEDS
½ TEASPOON SESAME OIL
½ TEASPOON SALT FLAKES

1 Preheat oven to 220°C/425°F. Line an oven tray with baking paper.
2 Combine ingredients in a medium bowl. Spread mixture onto tray.
3 Bake bean mixture for 15 minutes or until golden.

nutritional count per serving
7.5g total fat (0.6g saturated fat); 476kJ (114 cal); 6.6g carbohydrate; 6.1g protein; 0.2g fibre

tip You can use fresh or frozen (thawed) edamame; available from Asian food stores and some supermarkets. To quickly thaw the beans, place in a heatproof bowl, top with hot water; stand for 1 minute. Drain, then shell.

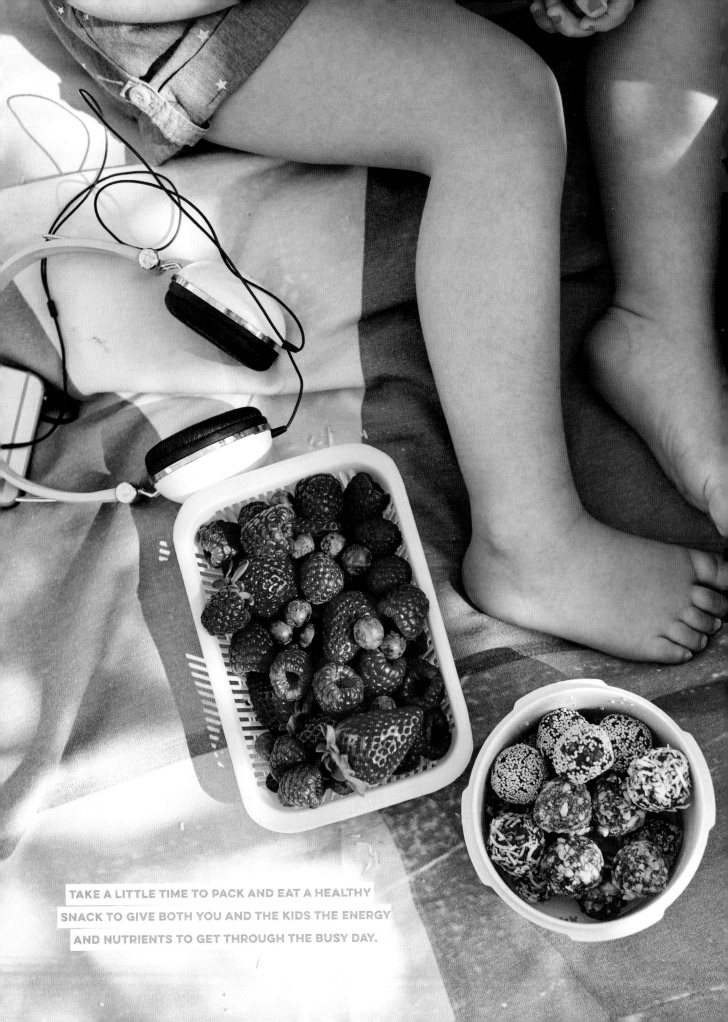

TAKE A LITTLE TIME TO PACK AND EAT A HEALTHY
SNACK TO GIVE BOTH YOU AND THE KIDS THE ENERGY
AND NUTRIENTS TO GET THROUGH THE BUSY DAY.

RAW
TURKISH DELIGHT BARK

PREP TIME **10 MINUTES (+ REFRIGERATION)** SERVES **10**

1 CUP (200G) VIRGIN COCONUT OIL
½ CUP (50G) CACAO POWDER
PINCH SEA SALT
⅓ CUP (115G) RICE MALT SYRUP
⅓ CUP (50G) COARSELY CHOPPED RAW ALMONDS
⅓ CUP (50G) DRIED CHERRIES
¼ CUP (4G) DRIED EDIBLE ROSE PETALS

1 Grease a 20cm x 30cm (8-inch x 12-inch) slice pan; line base and sides with baking paper, extending the paper 5cm (2-inches) over long sides of pan.

2 Place the oil, sifted cacao and salt in a medium bowl. Whisk to combine. Gradually add the syrup, whisking to combine.

3 Spread mixture evenly into pan. Scatter with nuts, cherries and rose petals. Refrigerate until set. Break into shards to serve.

nutritional count per serving
23.3g total fat (19.1g saturated fat); 1126kJ (269 cal); 14g carbohydrate; 2.4g protein; 0.4g fibre

tips Don't worry if the bark has a slight whitish look to it, this is simply the coconut fat, but it won't affect the taste. Because of the low melting point of the coconut oil, the bark should always be stored in the fridge otherwise it will be too soft to handle.

CACAO & HAZELNUT
COOKIES

PREP + COOK TIME **30 MINUTES** MAKES **16**

½ CUP (80G) FIRMLY PACKED
  FRESH DATES, PITTED
2 CUPS (200G) GROUND
  HAZELNUTS
1½ CUPS (225G) WHOLEMEAL
  SPELT FLOUR
¼ CUP (50G) CHIA SEEDS
1 TEASPOON GROUND
  CINNAMON
PINCH SEA SALT FLAKES
¼ CUP (50G) VIRGIN COCONUT
  OIL, AT ROOM TEMPERATURE
½ CUP (170G) RICE MALT SYRUP
1 FREE-RANGE EGG
2 TEASPOONS VANILLA EXTRACT
½ CUP (50G) CACAO NIBS

1 Preheat oven to 160°C/325°F. Line two oven trays with baking paper.
2 Place dates in a small heatproof bowl, cover with boiling water; stand for 5 minutes. Drain.
3 Process dates, ground hazelnuts, flour, seeds, cinnamon, salt, oil, syrup, egg and extract until well combined. Stir in cacao nibs.
4 Using damp hands, roll 2-tablespoonfuls of mixture into a ball, place on tray; flatten with the palm of your hand into a 6cm (2½-inch) round. Using the back of a damp fork, mark each cookie. Bake for 15 minutes or until a cookie can gently be pushed without breaking. Cool cookies on trays.

nutritional count per cookie
16.1g total fat (4g saturated fat); 1105kJ (264 cal); 22.7g carbohydrate; 5.9g protein; 2.7g fibre

tip Cacao nibs are created in the early stages of chocolate production; cocoa beans are dried then roasted, after which they are crushed into what is termed 'nibs'. The nibs are then ground to separate the cocoa butter and cocoa solids. Nibs are both textural and chocolatey with no sweetness. They can be found at health food stores and specialist food stores.

PEA, CHICKPEA &
HAZELNUT FALAFEL

PREP + COOK TIME **30 MINUTES (+ REFRIGERATION)** SERVES **4 (MAKES 12)**

½ CUP (60G) FROZEN PEAS, THAWED

125G (4 OUNCES) CANNED CHICKPEAS (GARBANZO BEANS), DRAINED, RINSED

50G (1½ OUNCES) FETTA, CRUMBLED

2 TABLESPOONS COARSELY CHOPPED FRESH MINT

1 FRESH LONG GREEN CHILLI, SEEDED, CHOPPED FINELY

1 EGG

¼ CUP (25G) GROUND HAZELNUTS

1 TABLESPOON WHITE SESAME SEEDS

¼ CUP (30G) FINELY CHOPPED HAZELNUTS

VEGETABLE OIL, FOR SHALLOW-FRYING

1 MEDIUM LEMON (140G), CUT INTO WEDGES

MINT YOGHURT

½ CUP (140G) GREEK-STYLE YOGHURT

1 TABLESPOON LEMON JUICE

1 TABLESPOON FINELY CHOPPED FRESH MINT

1 Place peas, chickpeas, fetta, mint, chilli, egg and hazelnut meal in a food processor; pulse until coarsely chopped and combined. Season. Shape tablespoons of mixture into balls; flatten slightly. Toss falafel in combined sesame seeds and chopped hazelnuts. Place falafel on an baking-paper-lined oven tray. Refrigerate for 30 minutes.

2 Meanwhile, make mint yoghurt.

3 Heat oil in a medium frying pan over medium-high heat; shallow-fry falafel, in batches, for 5 minutes or until golden brown. Drain on paper towel.

4 Serve falafel with mint yoghurt and lemon wedges.

mint yoghurt Combine ingredients in a small bowl.

nutritional count per serving
16.6g total fat (4.3g saturated fat); 990kJ (236 cal); 9.5g carbohydrate; 10.5g protein; 4.1g fibre

GINGER & SESAME
SEED LOGS

PREP + COOK TIME **15 MINUTES (+ REFRIGERATION)** MAKES **26**

1 CUP (100G) WALNUTS
1 CUP (140G) MACADAMIAS
1 CUP (90G) ROLLED OATS
400G (12½ OUNCES) FRESH
   MEDJOOL DATES, PITTED
1½ TEASPOONS GROUND GINGER
½ TEASPOON SEA SALT
½ CUP (75G) SESAME SEEDS

1 Process nuts and oats in a food processor until finely chopped. Add dates, ginger and salt; process until mixture forms a paste.
2 Shape level tablespoons of the mixture into 5cm (2-inch) long logs; place on a baking-paper-lined oven tray. Refrigerate for 15 minutes.
3 Meanwhile, stir sesame seeds in a frying pan over medium heat for 2 minutes or until lightly toasted. Leave to cool.
4 Roll logs in sesame seeds; place on a tray. Refrigerate for 2 hours or until firm.

nutritional count per log
8.6g total fat (0.9g saturated fat); 601kJ (143 cal); 14.5g carbohydrate; 2.3g protein; 1.2g fibre

tips Medjool dates are available from the fresh food section of major supermarkets. Store the logs in an airtight container in the fridge for up to 2 weeks or freeze for up to 3 months.

TOASTED
NORI CHIPS

PREP + COOK TIME **15 MINUTES** MAKES **ABOUT 60**

2 TEASPOONS SESAME SEEDS
1 TEASPOON SEA SALT,
CRUMBLED
10 NORI (SEAWEED) SHEETS
2 TABLESPOONS SESAME OIL
NANAMI TOGARASHI
1 TABLESPOON FINELY GRATED
ORANGE RIND
2 TEASPOONS CRACKED
BLACK PEPPER
1 TABLESPOON CHILLI FLAKES
2 TEASPOONS BLACK
SESAME SEEDS

1 Make nanami togarashi.
2 Crush sesame seeds using a mortar and pestle; combine with 2 teaspoons of the nanami togarashi and the salt. (Store remaining nanami togarashi for another use.)
3 Using scissors, cut each nori sheet into triangles or squares. Place on a large baking-paper-lined oven tray; lightly brush nori with sesame oil.
4 Heat a large non-stick frying pan over medium-high heat; toast nori, in batches, for 2 minutes each side or until crisp. Return to paper-lined tray; sprinkle immediately with nanami togarashi mixture.

nanami togarashi Dry-fry rind in a small frying pan over medium heat for 5 minutes or until rind is dry and crispy. Place in a screw-top jar with remaining ingredients; shake well to combine.

nutritional count per chip
0.6g total fat (0.1g saturated fat); 31kJ (7 cal); 0.1g carbohydrate; 0.2g protein; 0.02g fibre

tip Nanami togarashi is a Japanese seven-spice mix, also called shichimi togarashi (both nana and shichi mean seven in Japanese). The blend contains red peppers, sansho pepper, orange rind, black and white sesame seeds, seaweed and ginger. It is available from Asian food stores if you don't want to make your own.

ROASTED SWEET & SOUR
CHICKPEAS & BEANS

PREP + COOK TIME **1 HOUR** SERVES **4 (MAKES 2½ CUPS)**

2 X 400G (12½ OUNCES) CANNED CHICKPEAS (GARBANZO BEANS)

2 X 400G (12½ OUNCES) CANNED BUTTER BEANS

1 TABLESPOON EXTRA VIRGIN OLIVE OIL

1 TABLESPOON FINELY GRATED LIME RIND

2 TEASPOONS GROUND CUMIN

2 TEASPOONS GROUND CORIANDER

1 TEASPOON CHILLI FLAKES

1 TABLESPOON COCONUT SUGAR

1 Preheat oven to 220°C/425°F. Line an oven tray with baking paper.

2 Drain then rinse chickpeas and beans; place in a medium heatproof bowl. Cover with boiling water; drain. Dry on paper towel. (This will ensure that the chickpeas and beans will dry and crisp during roasting.)

3 Place chickpeas and beans on tray. Bake for 50 minutes, stirring occasionally, or until mixture is golden and crisp.

4 Transfer roasted chickpeas and beans to a medium bowl. Add oil, rind, cumin, coriander, chilli flakes and coconut sugar. Season with plenty of salt and freshly ground black pepper; toss until well coated.

nutritional count per serving
9.6g total fat (1.3g saturated fat); 1381kJ (330 cal); 37.4g carbohydrate; 17.9g protein; 15g fibre

tips You can use dried legumes instead of canned: soak them overnight first, then cook for 1½ hours in boiling water. Experiment with different spices and herbs to flavour how you like it. Store the roasted mix in an airtight container or jar for up to 4 days.

CHIA & TOMATO GUACAMOLE
WITH SUMAC CRISPS

PREP + COOK TIME **20 MINUTES** SERVES **4**

COOKING OIL SPRAY
4 RYE MOUNTAIN BREADS (100G)
1½ TEASPOONS GROUND SUMAC
2 MEDIUM AVOCADOS (500G),
  CHOPPED COARSELY
⅓ CUP (80ML) LIME JUICE
1 SMALL RED ONION (100G),
  CHOPPED FINELY
⅓ CUP (60G) SEMI-DRIED
  TOMATOES, CHOPPED FINELY
¼ CUP FRESH CORIANDER
  (CILANTRO) LEAVES, CHOPPED
½ TEASPOON SMOKED PAPRIKA
1½ TABLESPOONS BLACK OR
  WHITE CHIA SEEDS
2 FRESH LONG RED CHILLIES,
  SLICED THINLY

1 Preheat oven to 200°C/400°F. Line three oven trays with baking paper; spray with cooking oil.
2 Cut each sheet of mountain bread into 16 triangles. Place in a single layer on trays; spray with oil. Sprinkle with sumac; season with salt and pepper. Bake for 5 minutes or until golden and crisp.
3 Place avocado and juice in a medium bowl; mash lightly with a fork. Stir in red onion, tomato, coriander, paprika, 1 tablespoon chia seeds and three-quarters of the chilli. Season to taste with salt.
4 Place guacamole in a serving bowl; top with remaining chilli and remaining chia seeds. Serve with sumac crisps.

nutritional count per serving
23g total fat (4.7g saturated fat); 1391kJ (332 cal); 19g carbohydrate; 7.2g protein; 6.5g fibre

tips Guacamole can be stored, covered, in the fridge for up to 2 days. Sumac crisps will keep in an airtight container at room temperature for up to 1 week.

IF YOU FILL YOUR KITCHEN WITH GOOD FOOD, YOU WILL EAT GOOD FOOD. HEAD TO THE MARKETS ON THE WEEKENDS OR VISIT YOUR LOCAL GROCER AND KEEP A VARIETY OF FRESH, SEASONAL FRUIT AND VEGETABLES CLOSE AT HAND SO THEY'RE EASY TO INCLUDE IN YOUR MEALS AND SNACKS.

GREEN POWER
MINI FRITTATAS

PREP + COOK TIME **35 MINUTES** MAKES **8**

2 TEASPOONS OLIVE OIL

**1 SMALL LEEK (200G),
SLICED THINLY**

½ CLOVE GARLIC, CRUSHED

**3 CUPS (120G) FIRMLY PACKED
BABY SPINACH LEAVES,
CHOPPED FINELY**

5 EGGS

½ CUP (125ML) POURING CREAM

**1 TABLESPOON FINELY CHOPPED
FRESH MINT**

**1 TABLESPOON FINELY CHOPPED
FRESH BASIL**

**1 TABLESPOON FINELY CHOPPED
FRESH DILL**

**100G (3 OUNCES) GOAT'S FETTA,
CRUMBLED**

1 Preheat oven to 180°C/350°F. Line 8 holes of a 12-hole (⅓ cup/80ml) muffin pan with paper cases.

2 Heat oil in a medium saucepan over medium heat; cook leek, stirring, for 3 minutes. Add garlic; cook for 2 minutes or until leek is soft. Add spinach; cook, stirring, 30 seconds or until wilted. Remove from heat. Set aside.

3 Whisk eggs, cream and herbs in a medium jug; season.

4 Divide spinach mixture into pan holes; pour in egg mixture, then top with fetta.

5 Bake frittatas for 20 minutes or until set. Leave in pan for 5 minutes before serving warm or at room temperature.

nutritional count per frittata

12g total fat (6.4g saturated fat); 586kJ (140 cal); 0.9g carbohydrate; 6.6g protein; 0.7g fibre

tip Store frittatas in an airtight container in the fridge for up to 5 days or freeze for up to 1 month.

CREAMY CARROT
& MISO DIP

PREP + COOK TIME **20 MINUTES** SERVES **4**

2 SHEETS ORIGINAL MOUNTAIN
   BREAD (50G)
COOKING OIL SPRAY
2 MEDIUM CARROTS (260G),
   CHOPPED COARSELY
1 SMALL CLOVE GARLIC,
   CHOPPED
1 MEDIUM SHALLOT (25G),
   CHOPPED COARSELY
2 TABLESPOONS WHITE (SHIRO)
   MISO PASTE
¼ CUP (60ML) AVOCADO OR
   VEGETABLE OIL
2 TEASPOONS SESAME OIL
2 TABLESPOONS RICE
   WINE VINEGAR
1 TABLESPOON WATER
1 TEASPOON BLACK
   SESAME SEEDS
1 TABLESPOON MICRO
   CORIANDER (CILANTRO)
   LEAVES

1 Preheat oven to 200°C/400°F.
2 Place mountain bread on two
oven trays, spray both sides with
cooking oil; season with salt. Bake
for 4 minutes or until golden and
crisp. Break into large pieces.
3 Blend or process carrot, garlic,
shallot, miso, oils, vinegar and
the water for 30 seconds or until
mixture is smooth; season to taste.
4 Serve dip sprinkled with sesame
seeds and coriander, with mountain
bread crisps.

nutritional count per serving
18.1g total fat (2.6g saturated fat);
966kJ (231 cal); 12.1g carbohydrate;
3.3g protein; 3.5g fibre

*tips Mountain bread crisps will
keep in an airtight container
for up to 3 days. Store the dip
in an airtight container in the
fridge for up to 3 days; stir
before serving.*

FROZEN GREEN
POWER BITES

PREP + COOK TIME **10 MINUTES (+ FREEZING)** MAKES **25**

3 RIPE MEDIUM BANANAS (600G)
¼ CUP (30G) GROUND ALMONDS
½ CUP (70G) CHOPPED PITTED DATES
½ CUP (80G) CURRANTS
¾ CUP (90G) COARSELY CHOPPED PECANS
¼ CUP (35G) SESAME SEEDS
¼ CUP (25G) CACAO POWDER
2 TABLESPOONS COCONUT BUTTER (SEE TIPS), MELTED
½ CUP (40G) QUINOA FLAKES
1 TABLESPOON SPIRULINA POWDER (SEE TIPS)
2 TABLESPOONS BARLEY MALT SYRUP
25 MINI WOODEN POPSICLE STICKS
¼ CUP (20G) SHREDDED COCONUT
¼ CUP (30G) COARSELY CHOPPED PECANS, EXTRA

1 Mash banana in a large bowl with a fork. Add ground almonds, dates, currants, pecans, sesame seeds, cacao, coconut butter, quinoa flakes, spirulina powder and syrup; stir until well combined.

2 Spoon mixture into 25 ice-cube tray holes (2-tablespoon capacity). Insert popsicle sticks; freeze for 5 hours or until set.

3 Stir shredded coconut in a small frying pan over medium heat for 5 minutes or until golden. Transfer immediately to a small bowl; cool. Stir in extra pecans until combined.

4 Carefully ease power bites from holes; dip in coconut mixture. Store in an airtight container in the freezer until ready to eat.

nutritional count per bite
7.3g total fat (1g saturated fat); 486kJ (116 cal); 10g carbohydrate; 2.3g protein; 1.2g fibre

tips Coconut butter is the blended flesh of coconut. Spirulina is a cyanobacterium (sometimes referred to as blue-green algae although this is not technically correct) that grows in lakes. It is sold as a powder or as tablets. Spirulina powder is rich in protein and contains all the essential amino acids. It is a very good source of iron, is rich in B group vitamins, copper and manganese, as well as a source of the plant omega-3 fat, alpha-linolenic acid (ALA). Coconut butter and spirulina are both available from health food stores. Bites can be stored in the freezer for up to 1 month.

KALE CHIPS

PREP + COOK TIME **25 MINUTES (+ COOLING)** SERVES **8**

450G (14½ OUNCES) KALE
1 TABLESPOON EXTRA VIRGIN
 OLIVE OIL
½ TEASPOON CRUSHED
 SEA SALT FLAKES

1 Preheat oven to 190°C/375°F; place three large oven trays in the oven while preheating.

2 Remove and discard kale stems from leaves. Wash leaves well; pat dry with paper towel or in a salad spinner. Tear kale leaves into 5cm (2-inch) pieces; place in a large bowl, then drizzle with oil and sprinkle with salt. Using your hands, rub oil and salt through the kale.

3 Spread kale, in a single layer, on heated trays. Bake for 10 minutes. Remove any pieces of kale that are already crisp. Return remaining kale to the oven for a further 2 minutes; remove any pieces that are crisp. Repeat until all the kale is crisp. Leave to cool.

nutritional count per serving
2.3g total fat (0.3g saturated fat); 135kJ (32 cal); 1.2g carbohydrate; 0.9g protein; 1.2g fibre

tip These kale chips will keep in an airtight container for up to 2 weeks.

RAW CHOCOLATE
FROZEN BANANA TREATS

PREP + COOK TIME **15 MINUTES (+ FREEZING)** MAKES **24**

6 MEDIUM BANANAS (1.2KG)
24 MINI POPSICLE STICKS
½ CUP (100G) COCONUT OIL, MELTED
2 TABLESPOONS PURE MAPLE SYRUP
1½ TABLESPOONS RAW HONEY
1 CUP (100G) CACAO POWDER
¾ CUP (120G) ROASTED SALTED PEANUTS, CHOPPED FINELY

1 Line two trays with baking paper.
2 Peel and cut bananas into 4cm (1½-inch) pieces; place standing upright on a tray. Push a popsicle stick into each banana piece; freeze for 1 hour.
3 Stir coconut oil, maple syrup and honey in a small saucepan over a low heat until almost melted. Remove from heat; continue stirring until completely melted. Sift cacao into coconut oil mixture; whisk until smooth. Transfer to a small jug.
4 Place 1½ teaspoonfuls of chopped peanuts, apart, in small piles over remaining tray. Dip three-quarters of each banana into cacao mixture; stand upright on a pile of chopped peanuts. Freeze a further 30 minutes or until coating is set.

nutritional count per treat
7g total fat (4.3g saturated fat); 479kJ (114 cal); 10g carbohydrate; 2.8g protein; 1.1g fibre

tip Freeze these banana treats in an airtight container for up to 3 days.

RELAXING

BATHS

FOOT BATH

Combine 1 cup epsom salts, 1½ Tbsp bicarbonate of soda, 3 drops tea tree oil and 5 drops of peppermint oil. Add 2 scoops to a warm foot bath. Soak feet for 15 minutes. This mix soothes sore muscles, aides relaxation fight and contains antibacterial properties.

ALMOND & VANILLA
bubble bath

COMBINE ½ CUP LIGHT ALMOND OIL, ½ CUP MILD LIQUID BODY SOAP, ¼ CUP HONEY, 1 EGG WHITE AND 1 TABLESPOON VANILLA EXTRACT. POUR UP TO ½ CUP MIXTURE UNDER RUNNING WATER. STORE LEFTOVER MIXTURE IN THE FRIDGE.

Bath time
TEA BAGS

Adding a herbal blend to the tub, turns your bath into a giant cup of tea that helps reduce stress and soothe your aches. Keep sealed jars of the following mixes in the bathroom; scoop into a muslin pouch and add to your bath while the water is running.

To Relax: ½ cup oats, ½ cup lavender, ¼ cup dried orange rind strips, ½ cup chamomile, ¼ cup rosemary and 12 crushed bay leaves. *To Rejuvenate*: ½ cup rose petals, ½ cup lavender, ½ cup rosemary and ½ cup sage. *For a Peaceful Sleep*: ½ cup chamomile and ½ cup rose petals.

CLEOPATRA MILK & HONEY SOAK Combine 2 cups milk, 1 cup honey, 1 cup boiling water, ½ cup sea salt, 2 tablespoons bicarbonate of soda and 10 drops of vanilla essential oil. Pour into a warm bath. The milk softens and soothes the skin, while honey is an antibacterial healing agent. Add fresh rose petals to make this bath fit for a queen.

LEMON, CHIA & YOGHURT
CAKE POPS

PREP + COOK TIME **1 HOUR (+ STANDING)** MAKES **26**

You will need a 20-hole (1 tablespoon/20ml) silicone cake pop pan (see tips below). They are available from kitchen supply shops and online.

100G (3 OUNCES) UNSALTED BUTTER, SOFTENED

1 CUP (220G) NORBU (MONK FRUIT SUGAR)

2 EGGS

2 TABLESPOONS GREEK-STYLE YOGHURT

1 TABLESPOON FINELY GRATED LEMON RIND

2 TABLESPOONS LEMON JUICE

1 CUP (135G) GLUTEN-FREE PLAIN (ALL-PURPOSE) FLOUR

1½ TEASPOONS GLUTEN-FREE BAKING POWDER

½ TEASPOON XANTHAN GUM

1 TABLESPOON BLACK CHIA SEEDS

26 LOLLYPOP STICKS OR STRAWS

YOGHURT GLAZE

1 VANILLA BEAN

½ CUP (140G) GREEK-STYLE YOGHURT

2 TEASPOONS NATURAL LEMON EXTRACT

½ CUP (90G) STEVIA ICING MIX

1 Preheat oven to 200°C/400°F.

2 Beat butter and norbu in the small bowl of an electric mixer for 4 minutes or until light and fluffy; beat in eggs, one at a time. Add yoghurt, rind and juice; beat until just combined. Sift in flour, baking powder and xanthan gum; stir with a wooden spoon until combined.

3 Lightly grease the base of a 20-hole (1 tablespoon/20ml) silicone cake pop pan (see tips). Fill only the holes around the edge of one side of the pan with heaped 2 teaspoons of cake batter; the holes will look over full. Place pop pan lid on top tightly; bake for 18 minutes or until a toothpick inserted through one of the holes comes out clean. Cool in pan for 2 minutes; then pop cake pops out onto a wire rack. Cool. Repeat with remaining batter. Trim off any ragged edges with scissors.

4 Make yoghurt glaze.

5 Put the empty silicone pan together to become the holder. One at a time, insert a stick into the middle of each cake pop, dip into glaze then sprinkle with chia seeds; place in the holder while you finish the rest. To hold the extra cake pops, pierce holes in an egg carton with a wooden skewer. Serve cake pops in jars to keep them upright.

yoghurt glaze Split vanilla bean lengthways; scrape seeds into a small bowl. Add remaining ingredients; whisk to combine.

nutritional count per pop

4.1g total fat (2.4g saturated fat); 337kJ (81 cal); 8.6g carbohydrate; 1g protein; 0.1g fibre

tips Silicon cake pop moulds have two near identical sides. One half is filled, while the other with tiny holes at the top forms the lid. The mould is deliberately over filled for the mixture to rise to the other side and form a ball shape. We found even cooking was achieved by only filling the holes around the outside edge of the pan.

SWEET
POTATO CHIPS

PREP + COOK TIME **30 MINUTES** SERVES **8**

**2 SMALL PURPLE-SKINNED
WHITE SWEET POTATO (320G)
2 SMALL KUMARA (ORANGE
SWEET POTATO) (500G)
VEGETABLE OIL, FOR
DEEP-FRYING
SEA SALT FLAKES, TO SERVE**

1 Scrub vegetables lightly and wash well; pat dry. Trim ends of vegetables. Using a mandoline or V-slicer, slice vegetables lengthways into 1mm slices.

2 Preheat the oil in a large saucepan to 150°C/300°F. Deep-fry white sweet potato, in batches, until beginning to brown around the edges. Remove from oil with a slotted spoon; drain well on paper towel. When cooled, if any chips are not completely crisp, deep-fry again for 30 seconds; drain on paper towels. Repeat with kumara.

3 Sprinkle chips lightly with salt before serving.

nutritional count per serving
5.8g total fat (0.8g saturated fat); 611kJ (146 cal); 19.8g carbohydrate; 2.7g protein; 2.5g fibre

tip These chips will stay fresh in an airtight container for up to 2 days.

SEEDED
PARMESAN CRISPS

PREP + COOK TIME **30 MINUTES** MAKES **24**

2 CUPS (160G) FINELY GRATED PARMESAN
1 TABLESPOON WHITE CHIA SEEDS
1 TABLESPOON LINSEEDS (FLAXSEEDS)
1 TABLESPOON WHITE SESAME SEEDS

1 Preheat oven to 180°C/350°F. Line two large oven trays with baking paper.
2 Place level tablespoons of grated parmesan in mounds on trays. Flatten mounds to about 7.5cm (3 inches) in diameter, leaving 2.5cm (1 inch) between rounds. Combine seeds in a small bowl; sprinkle ½ teaspoon of seed mixture on each round. Season lightly with freshly ground black pepper.
3 Bake crisps for 12 minutes or until melted and lightly golden. Leave on trays to cool. Store in an airtight container.

nutritional count per crisp
2.8g total fat (1.4g saturated fat); 157kJ (37 cal); 0.1g carbohydrate; 2.8g protein; 0.2g fibre

tip Store crisps in an airtight container for up to 1 week.
serving suggestion Serve with cheese and olives. They would also work well crumbled over salads instead of croûtons.

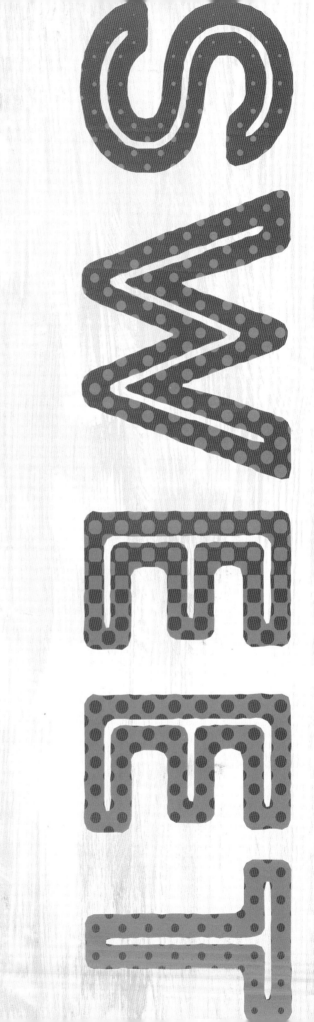

ORANGE & MINT
RICOTTA WITH RASPBERRIES

PREP + COOK TIME **20 MINUTES (+ REFRIGERATION)** SERVES **4**

1 MEDIUM ORANGE (240G)
1 CUP (240G) RICOTTA
½ CUP (140G) GREEK-STYLE YOGHURT
1 TABLESPOON FINELY CHOPPED FRESH MINT
250G (8 OUNCES) FRESH RASPBERRIES
2 TABLESPOONS SHELLED PISTACHIOS, CHOPPED
½ CUP FRESH MICRO MINT OR BABY MINT LEAVES
1 TABLESPOON HONEY

1 Using a vegetable peeler, peel rind from half the orange, avoiding any white pith. Cut rind into long thin strips; reserve. Finely grate remaining rind.

2 Press ricotta through a fine sieve into a medium bowl. Add yoghurt, grated rind and chopped mint; mix well. Refrigerate for 30 minutes.

3 Place reserved rind strips in a small heatproof bowl. Cover with boiling water; stand for 1 minute or until softened. Drain well.

4 Divide three quarters of the raspberries among four 1-cup (250ml) serving glasses; spoon ricotta mixture on berries. Top with pistachios, remaining raspberries, rind strips and baby mint leaves; drizzle with honey.

nutritional count per serving
9.7g total fat (4.7g saturated fat); 872kJ (208 cal); 18.4g carbohydrate; 8.9g protein; 5.1g fibre

tip You can use either fresh or packaged ricotta in this recipe.

DARK CHOCOLATE
& RICOTTA MOUSSE

PREP + COOK TIME **20 MINUTES** SERVES **6**

Unlike most chocolate mousse recipes, this one can be served just after it is made.

⅓ CUP (110G) RICE MALT SYRUP

1 TABLESPOON DUTCH-
    PROCESSED COCOA

2 TABLESPOONS WATER

½ TEASPOON VANILLA EXTRACT

200G (6½ OUNCES) DARK
    CHOCOLATE (70% COCOA),
    CHOPPED COARSELY

8 FRESH DATES (160G), PITTED

½ CUP (125ML) MILK

2 CUPS (480G) RICOTTA

2 TABLESPOONS POMEGRANATE
    SEEDS (SEE TIPS)

2 TABLESPOON CHOPPED
    PISTACHIOS

1 Stir syrup, cocoa, the water and extract in a small saucepan over medium heat; bring to the boil. Remove from heat; cool.

2 Place chocolate in a small heatproof bowl over a small saucepan of simmering water (don't let the water touch the base of the bowl); stir until melted and smooth.

3 Process dates and milk until dates are finely chopped. Add ricotta; process until smooth. Add melted chocolate; process until mixture is well combined.

4 Spoon mousse into six ¾ cup (180ml) serving glasses. Spoon cocoa syrup on mousse; top with pomegranate seeds and nuts.

nutritional count per serving
21g total fat (12g saturated fat); 2020kJ (482 cal); 62g carbohydrate; 12.3g protein; 3.8g fibre

tips Fresh pomegranate seeds can sometimes be found in the fridge section of supermarkets and greengrocers. To remove the seeds from a pomegranate, cut the fruit in half crossways; hold it, cut-side down, in the palm of your hand over a bowl, then hit the outside firmly with a wooden spoon. The seeds should fall out easily; discard any white pith that falls out with them. Pomegranate seeds will keep in the fridge for up to a week. You can make this mousse a day ahead; refrigerate, covered, then bring to room temperature before serving.

VEGAN BROWNIE
& STRAWBERRY CHEESECAKE

PREP TIME **20 MINUTES (+ FREEZING)** SERVES **10**

You will need to start this recipe the day before.

1½ CUPS (180G) PECANS
⅓ CUP (35G) DUTCH-PROCESSED COCOA
250G (8 OUNCES) FRESH DATES, PITTED
1 TEASPOON VANILLA EXTRACT
4 CUPS (560G) RAW MACADAMIA HALVES
500G (1 POUND) STRAWBERRIES, CHOPPED COARSELY
½ CUP (175G) RICE MALT SYRUP
¼ CUP (60G) COCONUT OIL
1 TABLESPOON VANILLA EXTRACT, EXTRA
2 TABLESPOONS WATER
250G (8 OUNCES) STRAWBERRIES, EXTRA, HALVED
2 TABLESPOONS RICE MALT SYRUP, EXTRA

1 Grease and line base and side of a 20cm (8-inch) springform pan with baking paper.
2 Process pecans and cocoa until roughly chopped. With the motor operating, gradually add dates and extract, processing until mixture resembles coarse crumbs and holds together when pressed. Press mixture onto base of pan using the back of a spoon. Freeze 30 minutes. Clean food processor bowl.
3 Process macadamias until roughly chopped. Add strawberries, syrup, solid coconut oil, extra extract and the water. Process for 2 minutes or until as smooth as possible. Pour mixture over brownie base. Freeze cheesecake for 4 hours or until very firm.
4 Using your hands, squeeze juice from 3 of the extra strawberries into a small bowl (discard pulp), add remaining extra strawberries and extra syrup; stir to combine. Just before serving, top cheesecake with strawberry mixture.

nutritional count per serving
62.2g total fat (12.4g saturated fat); 3173kJ (759 cal); 41g carbohydrate; 8.5g protein; 9.1g fibre

tip The cheesecake can be made and frozen up to 2 days ahead. Place in the fridge 15 minutes before serving to soften slightly.

SPELT CRÊPES WITH
POACHED PEAR
& BLUEBERRIES

PREP + COOK TIME **35 MINUTES (+ STANDING)** SERVES **4**

2 FREE-RANGE EGGS
1 CUP (250ML) MILK
⅓ CUP (50G) PLAIN (ALL-PURPOSE) SPELT FLOUR
⅓ CUP (50G) WHOLEMEAL PLAIN (ALL-PURPOSE) SPELT FLOUR
360G (11½ OUNCES) RICOTTA
2 TABLESPOONS PURE MAPLE SYRUP
1 TEASPOON GROUND CINNAMON
2 TEASPOONS COCONUT OIL
POACHED PEAR & BLUEBERRIES
½ CUP (125ML) RED WINE
½ CUP (125ML) FRESHLY SQUEEZED ORANGE JUICE
1 CINNAMON STICK
2 TABLESPOONS PURE MAPLE SYRUP
2 SMALL CORELLA PEARS (300G), UNPEELED
125G (4 OUNCES) BLUEBERRIES

1 Make poached pear and blueberries.
2 Meanwhile, process eggs, milk and flours until smooth. Transfer to a jug; stand for 20 minutes.
3 Whisk ricotta, maple syrup and cinnamon in a bowl until smooth.
4 Brush a heated 20cm (8-inch) crêpe pan with a little of the coconut oil. Pour scant ¼ cups of batter into pan, swirling to coat the base; cook 30 seconds or until browned underneath. Turn crêpe; cook further 10 seconds or until browned lightly underneath. Transfer to a plate; cover to keep warm. Repeat with remaining oil and batter to make 8 crêpes in total.
5 Spread 2 tablespoons of the ricotta mixture on one quarter of each crêpe; fold crêpe into quarters over the filling. Serve crêpes with poached fruit and poaching liquid.

poached pear & blueberries Bring wine, juice, cinnamon and syrup to the boil in a medium saucepan over medium heat. Meanwhile, quarter and core pears; cut into thin wedges. Add pears to wine mixture; simmer, uncovered, for 10 minutes or until tender. Add blueberries; remove pan from heat.

nutritional count per serving
15g total fat (9g saturated fat); 1836kJ (438 cal); 52g carbohydrate; 17g protein; 6.8g fibre

tips The cooking time of the pears will depend on their ripeness. Buy ricotta fresh from the deli; it should be moist.

SALTED COCONUT &
PASSIONFRUIT SEMIFREDDO

PREP + COOK TIME **30 MINUTES (+ FREEZING)** SERVES **10**

You need about 9 passionfruit for the amount of pulp required.

2 CUPS (500ML) COCONUT CREAM (SEE TIPS)

6 FREE-RANGE EGGS, SEPARATED

⅓ CUP (115G) HONEY OR PURE MAPLE SYRUP

2 TEASPOONS VANILLA EXTRACT

½ CUP (50G) COCONUT MILK POWDER

1 TEASPOON SEA SALT FLAKES

⅓ CUP (80ML) FRESH PASSIONFRUIT PULP

¼ CUP (60ML) FRESH PASSIONFRUIT PULP, EXTRA

½ CUP (25G) UNSWEETENED COCONUT FLAKES

1 TABLESPOON MICRO MINT OR SMALL FRESH MINT LEAVES

1 Pour coconut cream into a medium metal bowl; place in the freezer for 30 minutes or until chilled.

2 Grease a 20cm x 11.5cm x 9cm (8-inch x 4¾-inch x 3¾-inch) loaf pan. Line base and sides with baking paper, extending the paper 5cm (2-inches) over sides of pan.

3 Beat egg yolks, 2 tablespoons of the honey and extract in a small bowl with an electric mixer on high for 5 minutes or until thick and pale. Transfer to a large bowl.

4 Beat egg whites in a clean small bowl with an electric mixer until soft peaks form. Gradually add the remaining honey; beat until thick and glossy.

5 Whisk chilled coconut cream, coconut milk powder and salt until slightly thickened. Gently fold egg whites and coconut cream mixture into egg yolk mixture.

6 Pour mixture into pan; freeze for 1 hour or until mixture has thickened slightly. Swirl through passionfruit pulp. Return to freezer for at least 3 hours or overnight.

7 Before serving, stand semifreddo at room temperature for 5 minutes. Invert semifreddo onto a serving platter; top with extra passionfruit, coconut flakes and mint.

nutritional count per serving
17.7g total fat (14.1g saturated fat); 988kJ (236 cal); 13.5g carbohydrate; 5.6g protein; 2.5g fibre

tips Use a brand of coconut cream that states it is 100% natural on the label. Coconut cream that has 'emulsifying agents' added (it will state this on the label) may cause the semifreddo to separate into creamy and watery layers. You could also peel the flesh of fresh coconut with a vegetable peeler, if you like, and substitute it for the coconut flakes.

SUGAR-FREE COCONUT
CHOCOLATE BARS

PREP + COOK TIME **30 MINUTES (+ FREEZING & REFRIGERATION)** MAKES **16**

We used 99.8% sugar-free chocolate, available from health food stores and pharmacies.

2½ CUPS (190G) SHREDDED COCONUT
2 TEASPOONS STEVIA
⅔ CUP (160ML) COCONUT CREAM
2 TEASPOONS VANILLA EXTRACT
300G (6 OUNCES) SUGAR-FREE DARK CHOCOLATE, CHOPPED FINELY
50G (1½ OUNCES) BUTTER

1 Combine coconut, stevia, coconut cream and half the extract in a medium bowl. Divide mixture into 16 portions; shape each portion into a 6cm (2½-inch) log. Place logs on a baking-paper-lined oven tray. Freeze for 1 hour or until firm.
2 Place chocolate and butter in a small microwave-safe bowl. Microwave on HIGH (100%) in 30-second bursts, stirring, until melted and smooth. Add remaining extract; stir until smooth. Cool to room temperature.
3 Dip bars, one at a time, into chocolate mixture to evenly coat; allow excess to drain, then return to tray. Refrigerate for 30 minutes or until firm.

nutritional count per bar
20.8g total fat (14.9g saturated fat); 897kJ (214 cal); 2.7g carbohydrate; 2.3g protein; 0.1g fibre

tips Stevia comes from the leaf of a plant, so is promoted as a natural sweetener. It is processed into a white powder that can be used in a similar way to sugar. It has a minimal effect on blood glucose levels and has no kilojoules, so it can be a useful way to reduce your sugar intake. These bars can be stored in an airtight container in the fridge for up to 1 week.

HONEY & LIME
BAKED PERSIMMONS

PREP + COOK TIME **25 MINUTES** SERVES **4**

You can use either astringent or non-astringent persimmons in this recipe. If you use the astringent variety, it is best to scrape away the flesh from the skin when eating.

**4 PERSIMMONS (1KG),
   CUT INTO 6 WEDGES
1 LIME, SLICED THINLY
4CM (1½-INCH) PIECE FRESH
   GINGER (20G), SLICED THINLY
1½ TABLESPOONS HONEY
200G (6½ OUNCES)
   PASSIONFRUIT FROZEN
   YOGHURT
1 TABLESPOON LIME RIND STRIPS
   (SEE TIPS)**

1 Preheat oven to 200°C/400°F. Cut four 35cm (14-inch) pieces of baking paper.

2 Place pieces of paper lengthways in front of you then divide persimmon wedges among baking paper, placing them crossways in the centre. Top with lime slices and ginger; drizzle with honey. Bring short edges of paper together, fold over several times to secure, then tuck sides under to form a parcel. Place parcels on two oven trays.

3 Bake parcels for 15 minutes or until persimmon is soft. Open parcels to serve, topped with spoonfuls of frozen yoghurt and lime rind.

nutritional count per serving
3g total fat (1.7g saturated fat); 1197kJ (286 cal); 58g carbohydrate; 4g protein; 7.4g fibre

tips There are two types of persimmons available in autumn: astringent and non-astringent. The first, is heart shaped and is eaten very ripe, otherwise the taste is very astringent. The other, which is sometimes sold as fuji fruit (fuji being the Japanese word for persimmon) is squat and eaten crisp. Use a zester to make the lime rind strips. If you don't have one, finely grate the rind instead.

SUGAR-FREE CRANBERRY
CHOCOLATE
SNACK BARS

PREP + COOK TIME **50 MINUTES (+ COOLING)** MAKES **16 BARS**

We used 99.8% sugar-free chocolate, available from health food stores and pharmacies.

2½ CUPS (50G) PUFFED RICE
½ CUP (60G) PECAN NUTS, CHOPPED
⅓ CUP (65G) PEPITAS (PUMPKIN SEEDS)
¼ CUP (35G) DRIED UNSWEETENED CRANBERRIES, CHOPPED COARSELY
2 TABLESPOONS LSA (SEE TIPS)
1 TABLESPOON WHITE SESAME SEEDS
½ CUP (180G) HONEY
1 TEASPOON VANILLA EXTRACT
½ TEASPOON SALT FLAKES
45G (1½ OUNCES) SUGAR-FREE DARK CHOCOLATE, CHOPPED

1 Preheat oven to 150°C/300°F. Grease a 20cm (8-inch) square cake pan; line base and two sides with baking paper, extending the paper 5cm (2 inches) over the sides.
2 Combine puffed rice, nuts, pepitas, cranberries, LSA and sesame seeds in a large bowl.
3 Place honey, extract and salt in a small saucepan over medium heat; cook, stirring, for 2 minutes or until mixture just comes to a simmer. Pour honey mixture over dry ingredients; stir through until evenly coated. Cool for 5 minutes. Add chocolate; stir until combined. Transfer mixture to pan; pressing down firmly with the back of a spoon.
4 Bake for 30 minutes or until golden brown. Leave in pan to cool. Cut into 16 bars.

nutritional count per bar
6.9g total fat (1.3g saturated fat); 548kJ (131 cal); 14.6g carbohydrate; 2.2g protein; 0.7g fibre

tips LSA is a ground mixture of linseeds, sunflower seeds and almonds. It is available from supermarkets and health food stores. When measuring honey, lightly spray inside the measuring cup with oil first and the honey will slide out more easily.

CHOCOLATE HAZELNUT
BROWNIES

PREP + COOK TIME **45 MINUTES** MAKES **24**

1 CUP (340G) RICE MALT SYRUP

1 CUP (140G) DRIED PITTED DATES, CHOPPED COARSELY

¼ TEASPOON SEA SALT FLAKES

½ CUP (125ML) WATER

½ TEASPOON BICARBONATE OF SODA (BAKING SODA)

200G (6½ OUNCES) BUTTER, CHOPPED

3 FREE-RANGE EGGS

¾ CUP (75G) COCOA POWDER

¾ CUP (75G) GROUND HAZELNUTS

½ CUP (75G) BUCKWHEAT FLOUR

½ CUP (120G) SOUR CREAM

½ CUP (70G) WHOLE ROASTED PEELED HAZELNUTS, HALVED

1½ TEASPOONS COCOA POWDER, EXTRA

1 Preheat oven to 180°C/350°F. Grease a 20cm x 30cm (8-inch x 12-inch) slice pan; line base with baking paper, extending the paper 5cm (2-inches) over long sides.

2 Place syrup, dates, salt and the water in a small saucepan over low heat; simmer for 5 minutes or until dates are soft.

3 Stir soda into date mixture, transfer to a food processor; process until smooth. Return date mixture to pan; add butter, stir over medium heat until butter melts. Pour mixture into a large bowl; cool for 5 minutes.

4 Whisk in eggs, one at a time. Stir in sifted cocoa, ground hazelnuts, flour, sour cream and chopped nuts. Spread mixture into pan; level top.

5 Bake brownie for 30 minutes or until a skewer inserted into the centre comes out with moist crumbs attached. Cool in pan. Dust with extra cocoa, then cut into squares.

nutritional count per brownie

13.3g total fat (6.2g saturated fat); 861kJ (205 cal); 19.5g carbohydrate; 2.6g protein; 1.5g fibre

tip Despite its name, buckwheat is unrelated to wheat and is known as a seed or pseudo-cereal, making it safe for those on coeliac diets. It is also high in fibre and protein.

GOLDEN BEETROOT &
CARROT CAKES

PREP + COOK TIME **40 MINUTES** MAKES **8**

3 CUPS (300G) GROUND
HAZELNUTS

3 TEASPOONS BAKING POWDER

⅓ CUP (55G) SULTANAS

⅓ CUP (45G) COARSELY
CHOPPED ROASTED
HAZELNUTS

⅓ CUP (120G) HONEY

¼ CUP (60G) COCONUT OIL

1 TEASPOON VANILLA EXTRACT

1 TEASPOON MIXED SPICE

3 FREE-RANGE EGGS

1½ CUPS (175G) COARSELY
GRATED CARROT

1 CUP (50G) COARSELY GRATED
GOLDEN BEETROOT (BEETS)

VANILLA YOGHURT, TO SERVE
(OPTIONAL)

CANDIED BEETROOT

1 BUNCH BABY GOLDEN
BEETROOT (BEETS) (500G),
SCRUBBED AND TRIMMED

1½ CUPS (375ML) PURE
MAPLE SYRUP

1 Preheat oven to 180°C/350°F. Grease and line 8 holes of a 12-hole (¾ cup/180ml) straight sided, loose-based mini cheese cake pan.

2 Combine ground hazelnuts, baking powder, sultanas and hazelnuts in a medium bowl.

3 Whisk honey, coconut oil, extract, mixed spice and eggs in a medium bowl until smooth. Pour honey mixture over dry ingredients; mix well. Fold in grated carrot and beetroot. Spoon mixture into holes.

4 Bake cakes for 30 minutes or until a skewer inserted in the centre comes out clean. Leave cakes in pan for 5 minutes before transferring to a wire rack to cool.

5 Meanwhile, make candied beetroot.

6 Serve cakes topped with candied beetroot and yoghurt.

candied beetroot Using a mandoline or V-slicer, cut beetroot into very thinly slices. Place slices in a medium saucepan with maple syrup; cook over medium heat for 10 minutes or until beetroot is candied.

nutritional count per cake

35.9g total fat (8.7g saturated fat); 2651kJ (633 cal); 68.1g carbohydrate; 9.9g protein; 7g fibre

tip You will need 2 bunches (1kg) baby golden beetroot for this recipe: 1 bunch to get 1 cup grated amount, and 1 bunch for the candied beetroot.

COCONUT & VANILLA

PREP + COOK TIME **40 MINUTES** MAKES **12**

Preheat oven to 180°C/350°F. Line a 12-hole (⅓ cup/80ml) muffin pan with paper cases. Sift 2 cups spelt flour and 2 teaspoons baking powder into a medium bowl. Whisk 1 teaspoon vanilla extract (see tip), 1 cup yoghurt, ½ cup melted cooled virgin coconut oil, ½ cup pure maple syrup and 2 eggs in a medium jug. Pour over dry ingredients; stir with a fork to just combine. Spoon mixture into cases; top with 1 cup coconut flakes. Bake for 30 minutes or until a skewer inserted into the centre comes out clean.

tip Vanilla extract contains a tiny amount of refined sugar; if you prefer, either use the scraped seeds of a vanilla bean or vanilla bean powder available from health food stores.

PEACH & GINGER CRUMBLE

PREP + COOK TIME **40 MINUTES** MAKES **12**

Preheat oven to 180°C/350°F. Line a 12-hole (⅓ cup/80ml) muffin pan with paper cases. Sift 2 cups spelt flour, 2 teaspoons baking powder, 1½ teaspoons ground ginger and 1 teaspoon ground cinnamon into a medium bowl; stir in 2 small (250g) coarsely chopped peaches. Whisk 1 teaspoon vanilla extract (see previous tip), 1 cup yoghurt, ½ cup melted cooled virgin coconut oil, ½ cup pure maple syrup and 2 eggs in a medium jug. Pour over dry ingredients; stir with a fork to just combine. Spoon mixture into cases. Place ⅓ cup coconut sugar, ½ cup spelt flour and 1 teaspoon ground cinnamon in a small bowl; rub in 60g (2oz) chopped cold unsalted butter until mixture resembles coarse crumbs. Sprinkle crumble on muffins. Bake for 30 minutes or until a skewer inserted into the centre comes out clean.

SUGAR FREE MUFFINS

10AM BOOST

TEA TIME

LEMON, THYME & FETTA

PREP + COOK TIME **40 MINUTES** MAKES **12**

Preheat oven to 180°C/350°F. Line a 12-hole (⅓ cup/80ml)
muffin pan with paper cases. Sift 2 cups spelt flour and
2 teaspoons baking powder into a medium bowl; stir in
2 teaspoons finely grated lemon rind and 1 tablespoon
finely chopped fresh thyme. Whisk 1¼ cups yoghurt,
½ cup melted cooled virgin coconut oil, ¼ cup pure
maple syrup and 2 eggs in a medium jug. Pour over
dry ingredients; stir with a fork until almost combined.
Fold through ½ cup crumbled goat's fetta. Spoon mixture
into cases; top with combined ⅔ cup crumbled goat's fetta,
⅓ cup pepitas and 2 tablespoons fresh thyme leaves.
Bake for 30 minutes or until a skewer inserted into
the centre comes out clean.

tip You could use regular fetta, if you prefer.

CHOC, BEETROOT & WALNUT

PREP + COOK TIME **40 MINUTES** MAKES **12**

Preheat oven to 180°C/350°F. Line a 12-hole (⅓ cup/80ml)
muffin pan with paper cases. Sift 2 cups spelt flour,
⅓ cup cacao powder and 2½ teaspoons baking powder
into a medium bowl. Coarsely grate 1 medium (130g)
washed, unpeeled beetroot (beet). Place beetroot in a
jug with 1½ cups yoghurt, ½ cup melted cooled virgin
coconut oil, ½ cup pure maple syrup and 2 eggs; whisk
with a fork to combine. Pour over dry ingredients; stir
with the fork until almost combined. Fold in 8 pitted
and coarsely chopped fresh medjool dates and ½ cup
chopped roasted walnuts. Spoon mixture into cases.
Bake for 30 minutes or until a skewer inserted into
the centre comes out clean.

LUNCH TREAT

3PM SLUMP

WATERMELON & LEMON
TEA GRANITA

PREP TIME **20 MINUTES (+ FREEZING)** SERVES **6**

You need to make this recipe the day before serving.

1 HERBAL LEMON TEA BAG
1 CUP (250ML) BOILING WATER
1 TABLESPOON POWDERED STEVIA OR NORBU (MONK FRUIT SUGAR)
500G (1 POUND) SEEDLESS WATERMELON, CHOPPED
1½ TABLESPOONS LEMON JUICE
600G (1¼ POUNDS) SEEDLESS WATERMELON, EXTRA, SLICED THINLY
FENNEL SALT
1 TABLESPOON SEA SALT FLAKES
1 TEASPOON FENNEL SEEDS
1 TEASPOON FINELY GRATED LEMON RIND

1 Steep the tea bag in the boiling water for 10 minutes; discard tea bag. Stir stevia into tea until dissolved.

2 Blend or process the watermelon until smooth. Stir in tea and lemon juice. Pour into a 2.5-litre (10-cup) shallow dish.

3 Freeze granita for 1 hour. Using a fork, break up any ice crystals. Freeze for a further 6 hours, scraping with a fork every hour or until frozen.

4 Make fennel salt.

5 Divide extra watermelon among serving glasses, top with granita and fennel salt.

fennel salt Using a pestle and mortar, crush ingredients together. (Alternatively, place in a small bowl and crush with the back of a wooden spoon.)

nutritional count per serving
0.3g total fat (0g saturated fat); 134kJ (32 cal); 6.3g carbohydrate; 0.5g protein; 0.7g fibre

tips Stevia and norbu are both natural sweeteners available from major supermarkets. Top each serving with thin strips of lemon or orange rind, if you like.

SLOW-ROASTED ROSE &
VANILLA QUINCE
GALETTE

PREP + COOK TIME **6 HOURS (+ COOLING)** SERVES **6**

Quince can be prepared to the end of step 4, up to 3 days ahead. Refrigerate, covered, until ready to continue with the rest of the recipe.

3 MEDIUM QUINCE (1KG)
¼ CUP (90G) HONEY
3 CUPS (750ML) WATER
1½ CUPS (375ML) ROSÉ WINE
1 CINNAMON STICK
1 VANILLA BEAN, SPLIT LENGTHWAYS INTO THIRDS
6 SHEETS FILLO PASTRY
2 TABLESPOONS EXTRA VIRGIN OLIVE OIL
1 TEASPOON GROUND CINNAMON
⅓ CUP (75G) LOW GI CASTER SUGAR (SUPERFINE SUGAR)
⅓ CUP (40G) GROUND ALMONDS
¼ CUP (40G) ROASTED ALMONDS, CHOPPED
1 CUP (280G) VANILLA BEAN GREEK-STYLE YOGHURT

1 Preheat oven to 150°C/300°F.

2 Peel quince; reserve half the peel. Cut quince into quarters, do not core.

3 Stir honey, the water, wine, cinnamon and vanilla in a large cast iron casserole or baking dish over medium heat until honey dissolves. Add quince and reserved peel, bring to the boil; cover with a piece of baking paper then cover tightly with foil, or a lid (make sure quince is submerged in the liquid).

4 Bake quince for 5 hours, turning twice, until quince are tender and deep red in colour. Leave quince in syrup to cool.

5 Remove quince from syrup with a slotted spoon. Cut cores from quince; cut each quarter in half lengthways. Strain syrup; reserve vanilla bean, discard peel. Reserve 2 cups (500ml) of the syrup. Return quince to remaining syrup; stand until required. Place reserved syrup in a saucepan over medium heat; simmer for 5 minutes or until thickened. Cool.

6 Preheat oven to 210°C/420°F. Grease a large oven tray; place tray in oven while heating.

7 Layer pastry sheets in alternate directions, on a large piece of baking paper, brushing each layer with some of the oil.

8 Combine cinnamon and sugar in a small bowl; reserve 2 tablespoons cinnamon sugar. Combine ground almonds with remaining cinnamon sugar. Sprinkle almond mixture over pastry leaving a 10cm (4-inch) border. Top with drained quince, fold edges of pastry over quince. Transfer galette, on baking paper, to preheated tray. Brush pastry with remaining oil; sprinkle pastry with reserved cinnamon sugar.

9 Bake galette for 20 minutes or until pastry is golden. Drizzle with reduced syrup, top with chopped almonds and reserved vanilla beans; serve with yoghurt.

nutritional count per serving
16.4g total fat (3g saturated fat); 1985kJ (474 cal); 60.9g carbohydrate; 6.9g protein; 10.3g fibre

CINNAMON & FIG
BAKED APPLES

PREP + COOK TIME **40 MINUTES** SERVES **6**

¼ CUP (35G) ROASTED
  HAZELNUTS, PEELED
3 DRIED FIGS
6 PITTED PRUNES
½ TEASPOON GROUND
  CINNAMON
1 TEASPOON VANILLA EXTRACT
6 LARGE RED APPLES (1.2KG),
  CORED (SEE TIP)
RICOTTA CREAM
1 CUP (240G) FRESH FIRM
  RICOTTA
½ CUP (125ML) MILK
1 TEASPOON VANILLA EXTRACT
½ TEASPOON FINELY GRATED
  MANDARIN RIND
MAPLE SAUCE
2 LARGE MANDARINS (500G)
¼ CUP (60ML) PURE MAPLE
  SYRUP
30G (1 OUNCE) COLD BUTTER,
  CHOPPED FINELY

1 Preheat oven to 160°C/325°F. Line oven tray with baking paper.
2 Process hazelnuts, figs, prunes, cinnamon and extract until coarsely chopped.
3 Using a small, sharp knife, score around the centre of each apple. Press hazelnut mixture into the cavities of each apple; place apples upright on tray. Bake for 30 minutes or until apples are tender.
4 Meanwhile, make ricotta cream, then maple sauce.
5 Serve apples with ricotta cream and maple sauce.

ricotta cream Process ricotta, milk and extract until smooth; stir in rind.
maple sauce Squeeze juice from mandarins; you will need ⅔ cup. Place juice and maple syrup in a small saucepan over medium heat; simmer until reduced by half and mixture is syrupy. Remove pan from heat; whisk in butter a few pieces at a time, until melted and combined.

nutritional count per serving
13.2g total fat (6.4g saturated fat); 1683kJ (402 cal); 61g carbohydrate; 7.9g protein; 5.6g fibre

tip We used royal gala apples in this recipe.

EVERY TIME
YOU EAT IS
AN OPPORTUNITY
TO NOURISH YOUR
BODY.

RASPBERRY & VANILLA
YOGHURT ICE-BLOCKS

PREP + COOK TIME **25 MINUTES (+ COOLING & FREEZING)** MAKES **14**

¼ CUP (55G) LOW-GI CANE
  SUGAR
1 VANILLA BEAN, SPLIT
  LENGTHWAYS
¾ CUP (180ML) WATER
300G (9½ OUNCES) FROZEN
  RASPBERRIES
750G (1½ POUNDS) GLUTEN-FREE
  LOW-FAT PLAIN YOGHURT

1 Stir sugar, vanilla bean and the water in a small saucepan over low heat for 4 minutes or until sugar is dissolved. Bring to the boil without stirring. Reduce heat; simmer for 10 minutes or until syrupy. Remove vanilla bean; leave syrup to cool.

2 Blend cooled syrup and raspberries until smooth. Very gently swirl in the yoghurt. Pour the mixture into 14 x ⅓ cup (80ml) ice-block moulds. Freeze overnight or until firm.

nutritional count per ice-block
0.2g total fat (0.1g saturated fat); 229kJ (55 cal); 8.3g carbohydrate; 3.5g protein; 1.3g fibre

tips Don't stir the yoghurt into the raspberry mixture or you will lose the marbled effect; it will swirl naturally when you pour the mixture into the moulds. Use a skewer to swirl it once in the moulds, if necessary. You could use frozen cherries, strawberries or mango instead of the raspberries, if you like.

COCONUT & MANGO
POPSICLES

PREP + COOK TIME **25 MINUTES (+ FREEZING)** MAKES **8**

1¾ CUPS (265G) FROZEN
  DICED MANGO
½ CUP (125ML) PURE FRESH
  APPLE JUICE
2 TABLESPOONS NORBU
  (MONK FRUIT SUGAR)
¼ CUP (60ML) WATER
270ML COCONUT CREAM
½ TEASPOON SEA SALT FLAKES
8 POPSICLE STICKS
¼ CUP (10G) COCONUT FLAKES,
  TOASTED

1 Process mango and apple juice until smooth. Place 2 tablespoons mango puree into each of eight ½-cup (125ml) popsicle moulds; freeze for 30 minutes.

2 Meanwhile, stir norbu and the water in a small saucepan over low heat until sugar dissolves (do not allow to simmer or boil or the mixture will crystallise). Whisk sugar syrup, coconut cream and salt to combine. Spoon mixture into popsicle moulds to fill. Cover moulds with a double layer of plastic wrap; this will help to keep the popsicle sticks upright. Pierce the plastic with a small knife, then push the popsicle sticks into each hole. Freeze for at least 4 hours or overnight.

3 Dip popsicle moulds briefly in boiling water; remove popsicles. Place toasted coconut in a small bowl, dip each popsicle quickly in hot water then into the coconut. Freeze on a baking-paper-lined tray for 10 minutes or until ready to eat.

nutritional count per popsicle
8.8g total fat (7.8g saturated fat); 461kJ (110 cal); 6.4g carbohydrate; 0.9g protein; 0.7g fibre

GLUTEN-FREE ZUCCHINI & BLUEBERRY LOAF CAKES

PREP + COOK TIME **45 MINUTES** MAKES **8**

3 MEDIUM ZUCCHINI (360G), GRATED COARSELY

2¾ CUPS (300G) GROUND ALMONDS

¾ CUP (120G) COCONUT SUGAR

1 TEASPOON GROUND CINNAMON

½ TEASPOON SEA SALT

2 TEASPOONS GLUTEN-FREE BAKING POWDER

½ CUP (175G) PURE MAPLE SYRUP

½ CUP (125ML) MELTED VIRGIN COCONUT OIL

3 EGGS, BEATEN LIGHTLY

1 VANILLA BEAN, SPLIT LENGTHWAYS, SEEDS SCRAPED

2 TEASPOONS FINELY GRATED ORANGE RIND

⅓ CUP (80ML) ORANGE JUICE

1 CUP (150G) FROZEN BLUEBERRIES

½ CUP (25G) COCONUT FLAKES, TOASTED

1 Preheat oven 180°C/350°F. Grease an 8-hole (½ cup/125ml) loaf pan tray; line base and long sides of holes with strips of baking paper, extending the paper 3cm (1¼-inches) over the long sides.

2 Squeeze liquid from zucchini; place zucchini in a large bowl. Add ground almonds, coconut sugar, cinnamon, salt and baking powder; stir to combine.

3 Whisk maple syrup, coconut oil, egg, vanilla seeds (reserve pod for another use), rind and juice in a small bowl. Add syrup mixture to zucchini mixture; stir gently to combine. Fold in blueberries. Spoon mixture into pan holes.

4 Bake loaves for 30 minutes or until risen and slightly cracked on top. Leave in pan for 5 minutes before turning, top-side up, onto a wire rack to cool.

5 Brush loaves with a little extra maple syrup; sprinkle with toasted coconut flakes.

nutritional count per loaf

39.2g total fat (16.3g saturated fat); 2227kJ (532 cal); 34.5g carbohydrate; 10.7g protein; 4.4g fibre

tips You can use any nut meal in this gluten-free recipe. Swap the blueberries for raspberries, if you prefer. Store these cakes in an airtight container for up to 3 days or in the freezer for up to 1 month.

WATERMELON SALAD
WITH ROSEHIP SYRUP

PREP + COOK TIME **40 MINUTES** SERVES **4**

**4 ROSEHIP AND HIBISCUS
  TEA BAGS**
⅔ CUP (160ML) HOT WATER
1 TABLESPOON RAW HONEY
2 TABLESPOONS ROSEWATER
**800G (1½ POUNDS) PIECE
  SEEDLESS WATERMELON**
4 MEDIUM NECTARINES (480G)
500G (1 POUND) STRAWBERRIES
**⅓ CUP (45G) PISTACHIOS,
  CHOPPED COARSELY**
**¼ CUP LOOSELY PACKED
  FRESH MINT LEAVES,
  CHOPPED FINELY**
**1 TABLESPOON MICRO BASIL OR
  SMALL FRESH MINT LEAVES,
  EXTRA**

1 Place tea bags in a heatproof jug, cover with the hot water; steep for 30 minutes. Discard tea bags. Place tea with honey in a small heavy-based saucepan, bring to a simmer over medium-high heat; cook for 8 minutes or until reduced to a thick syrup. Remove from heat; stir in rosewater, cool.

2 Meanwhile, remove rind from watermelon and cut flesh into small wedges. Halve and remove stones from nectarines; slice thinly. Halve strawberries.

3 Place chopped fruit in a large bowl with ¼ cup of the pistachios and the chopped mint; toss gently to combine. Drizzle with rosehip syrup; serve topped with remaining pistachios and extra mint.

nutritional count per serving
6.5g total fat (0.8g saturated fat); 955kJ (228 cal); 32g carbohydrate; 6g protein; 6.6g fibre

HAIR
TREATMENTS

HOT OIL INTENSE
moisture treatment

STIR 2 TABLESPOONS EXTRA VIRGIN COCONUT OIL, 2 TABLESPOONS EXTRA VIRGIN OLIVE OIL, 2 TABLESPOONS ALMOND OIL AND 2 TABLESPOONS JOJOBA OIL IN A SMALL SAUCEPAN OVER LOW HEAT UNTIL JUST LUKEWARM (DO NOT OVERHEAT OR YOU WILL BURN YOUR SCALP). MASSAGE WARM OIL ONTO YOUR SCALP AND HAIR, THEN WRAP HAIR TIGHTLY WITH A TOWEL. LEAVE ON YOUR HAIR FOR 30 MINUTES. RINSE OUT WITH WARM WATER AND A MILD SHAMPOO. TREATMENT CAN BE APPLIED ONCE A WEEK. THIS INTENSE MOISTURE TREATMENT WILL GIVE YOU SOFT SILKY TRESSES.

EGG WASH
FOR DRY HAIR

Using raw egg is a great way to give your hair a moisturising protein treatment, whilst the white contains bacteria-eating enzymes that removes unwanted oils. Wash clean, damp hair with ½ cup of egg mixture (whole egg – moisturises/conditions all hair types, egg whites – oily hair only, egg yolk – moisturises dry/brittle hair). Rinse out with cold water and shampoo as per normal. Treatment can be applied once per month.

FIX DULL
Hair

Mash ½ small avocado, 1 tablespoon extra virgin olive oil and ½ cup honey until smooth. Massage into clean, damp hair; leave on for about 20 minutes. Rinse out with hot water, then cold water. Treatment can be applied once a month and is great for dry, heat or UV-damaged hair. The protein-rich avocado helps restore and strengthen keratin bonds in the hair fibres, while honey attracts and locks in moisture.

ANTI-FRIZZ *Whisk 1 tsp jojoba oil, 1 tsp glycerin and 2 Tbsp aloe gel; stir in 5-10 drops lavender essential oil. Pour into a spray bottle with enough distilled water for your desired consistency. Store bottle in the firdge and shake well before use. This spray will smoothe and hydrate your hair.*

SQUASHED PLUM & RICOTTA
SANDWICHES

PREP + COOK TIME **15 MINUTES** MAKES **4**

You will need a sandwich press with two flat elements.

- **2 TABLESPOONS MELTED COCONUT OIL**
- **2 TEASPOONS SUGAR-FREE ICING MIX (SEE TIP)**
- **1 TEASPOON GROUND GINGER**
- **4 MEDIUM BLOOD PLUMS (340G), HALVED, STONES REMOVED**
- **1 TABLESPOON PURE MAPLE SYRUP**
- **8 X 2CM (¾-INCH) SLICES SOURDOUGH BREAD**
- **1 CUP (240G) FIRM RICOTTA**

1 Preheat a sandwich press. Brush press with half the coconut oil.

2 Combine icing mix and ginger in a small bowl.

3 Place plums, cut-side down, in the sandwich press. Cook, pressing down on the lid occasionally, for 6 minutes or until plums are tender and browned. Remove plums; wipe sandwich press clean.

4 Meanwhile, combine maple syrup and remaining coconut oil in a small bowl. Brush oil mixture over one side of each piece of bread.

5 Place four slices of bread, oiled-side down, on a board; spread with ricotta and top with plums. Top with remaining bread slices, oiled-side up.

6 Cook in sandwich press, in two batches, for 3 minutes or until golden brown and heated through. Serve sandwiches immediately, dusted with ginger icing mix.

nutritional count per sandwich

17.3g total fat (13g saturated fat); 1565kJ (374 cal); 39g carbohydrate; 13g protein; 3.9g fibre

tip We used Natvia icing mix made from stevia. It is available in the baking aisle from most supermarkets.

PEACH & PISTACHIO
CAKE POTS

PREP + COOK TIME **45 MINUTES** MAKES **12**

4 SMALL PEACHES (460G), HALVED

1 CUP (280G) GREEK-STYLE YOGHURT

2 MEDIUM APPLES (300G), GRATED COARSELY

2 EGGS, BEATEN LIGHTLY

¼ CUP (60ML) MILK

2 TABLESPOONS RAW HONEY

2 CUPS (240G) GROUND ALMONDS

2 TEASPOONS GLUTEN-FREE BAKING POWDER

⅓ CUP (45G) PISTACHIOS, CHOPPED COARSELY

1½ TABLESPOONS RAW HONEY, EXTRA

1 Preheat oven to 180°C/350°F. Cut 12 x 12cm (4-inch) squares from baking paper; line 12 x ⅓ cup (80ml) ovenproof pots with paper squares (see tips).

2 Thinly slice three of the peaches. Coarsely chop remaining peach; blend or process to a coarse puree. Fold peach puree through yoghurt in a small bowl; cover and refrigerate until required.

3 Place apple, egg, milk, honey, ground almonds and baking powder in a large bowl; mix until just combined. Spoon mixture into pots; push peach slices 2cm (¾-inch) into the top of the batter.

4 Bake cakes for 30 minutes or until a skewer inserted in the centre comes out clean. Top cakes with pistachios; drizzle with extra honey. Serve warm or at room temperature with peach yoghurt.

nutritional count per cake
13.8g total fat (1.1g saturated fat); 813kJ (194 cal); 10g carbohydrate; 6.3g protein; 3g fibre

tips We used peat seedling pots available from hardware stores and garden nurseries. You can also cook the cakes in a 12-hole (¹/₃ cup/80ml) muffin pan, lined with baking paper squares. This recipe is best made on the day of serving.

APRICOT & HAZELNUT
CRUMBLE

PREP + COOK TIME **1 HOUR** SERVES **4**

4 MEDIUM APRICOTS (325G)

2 MEDIUM PEARS (460G)

80G (2½ OUNCES) DRIED FIGS

10G (½ OUNCE) BUTTER

¾ CUP (180ML) WATER

½ CUP (125ML) PURE MAPLE SYRUP

¾ CUP (60G) QUINOA FLAKES

¼ CUP (30G) GROUND HAZELNUTS

½ CUP (70G) COARSELY CHOPPED SKINLESS HAZELNUTS, ROASTED

½ TEASPOON SEA SALT FLAKES

1 CUP (280G) GREEK-STYLE YOGHURT

2 TEASPOONS LONG THIN STRIPS ORANGE RIND

1 Preheat oven to 180°C/350°F.

2 Cut apricots in half; remove and discard stones. Cut unpeeled pears in half; remove core and cut each half into three wedges. Remove stem end from figs and quarter.

3 Combine apricot, pear, fig, butter and the water in a medium saucepan over medium heat; cook, stirring occasionally, for 6 minutes or until pears have softened slightly. Transfer fruit mixture to a 1.5 litre (6-cup) ovenproof dish.

4 Combine maple syrup, quinoa flakes, ground hazelnuts, chopped hazelnuts and salt in a medium bowl; sprinkle over fruit.

5 Bake crumble for 45 minutes or until top is lightly golden. Serve warm topped with yoghurt and rind.

nutritional count per serving

22.9g total fat (4.9g saturated fat); 2295kJ (549 cal); 71.5g carbohydrate; 10.6g protein; 9.9g fibre

tip If you prefer, use 3 peaches instead of the pears; ground almonds instead of ground hazelnuts; chopped almonds instead of hazelnuts; and raw honey instead of maple syrup.

COCONUT FRITTERS
WITH MANGO, CHILLI & LIME

PREP + COOK TIME **50 MINUTES** SERVES **4**

1 YOUNG DRINKING COCONUT (1.2KG)
2 MEDIUM BANANAS (400G), MASHED
¼ CUP (60ML) COCONUT CREAM
⅔ CUP (100G) PLAIN (ALL-PURPOSE) FLOUR
1 TEASPOON BAKING POWDER
¾ CUP (60G) SHREDDED COCONUT
2½ TABLESPOONS COCONUT NECTAR OR AGAVE SYRUP
RICE BRAN OIL, FOR DEEP-FRYING
2 TABLESPOONS LIME JUICE
1 MEDIUM MANGO (430G), SLICED THINLY
1½ TABLESPOONS FINELY GRATED LIME RIND
1 FRESH LONG RED CHILLI, SEEDED, SLICED THINLY

1 Insert the tip of a small knife into the soft spot on the base of the coconut, using a twisting action. Place coconut over a glass; drain coconut water (reserve for another use). Wrap coconut in a clean towel, break open with a hammer, or by smashing it onto the floor. Spoon out the soft coconut flesh; you should have about ½ cup (90g) of the flesh. Thinly slice coconut flesh.
2 Combine fresh coconut, banana, coconut cream, ½ cup of the flour, baking powder, ¼ cup of the shredded coconut and 2 teaspoons of the coconut nectar in a large bowl.
3 Combine remaining flour and shredded coconut in a medium bowl. Roll level tablespoons of coconut mixture into balls. Roll balls in flour mixture.

4 Fill a wok one-third with oil and heat to 160°C/325°F (or until a cube of bread browns in 25-30 seconds). Deep-fry coconut balls, in batches, for 2½ minutes or until golden and cooked through. Drain on paper towel.
5 Meanwhile, combine juice and remaining coconut nectar in a small bowl; stir in mango, rind and chilli.
6 Serve fritters with mango mixture and syrup.

nutritional count per serving
28.8g total fat (17.1g saturated fat); 2169kJ (519 cal); 55.8g carbohydrate; 6.4g protein; 8.3g fibre

TURMERIC & HONEY TONIC

PREP + COOK TIME **15 MINUTES**

SERVES **2 (MAKES 2 CUPS)**

Place 2 cups unsweetened almond milk, 1 tablespoon raw honey, 2 teaspoons grated fresh turmeric, 1 cinnamon stick and 4 slices fresh ginger in a small saucepan over low-medium heat; bring almost to the boil. Remove from heat; set aside for 10 minutes to allow flavours to infuse. Strain through a fine sieve into heatproof glasses; dust with a pinch of ground cinnamon.

tip You can use your favourite nut milk or other milk, if you prefer.

HOT! CHOCOLATE

PREP + COOK TIME **20 MINUTES**

SERVES **2 (MAKES 3 CUPS)**

Split a vanilla bean lengthways; scrape seeds into a small saucepan, add vanilla pod. Cut 1 fresh long red chilli into four. Add three pieces to the pan; thinly slice remaining piece, reserve to serve. Add 3 cups coconut milk blend (see tip) to the pan; bring to the boil. Remove from heat; stand 5 minutes. Discard chilli and bean. Stir 2 tablespoons raw cacao powder and 1 tablespoon rice malt syrup into infused milk; simmer, stirring, 2 minutes or until cacao is dissolved and milk heated through. Top with remaining chilli.

tip We used Pureharvest Coco Quench a blend of coconut and rice milks; it has a thinner consistency than canned coconut milk, but still has a great coconut milk taste.

HOT DRINKS

TUMMY SOOTHER

SPICY CHOC

TURKISH NIGHT CAP

PREP + COOK TIME **10 MINUTES**
SERVES **2 (MAKES 1½ CUPS)**

Stir 2 cups milk, 1 tablespoon raw honey and
2 cinnamon sticks in a small saucepan over low-medium
heat; simmer, without boiling, for 10 minutes. Remove from
heat; stand for 10 minutes. Discard cinnamon. Return pan
to low heat; simmer 5 minutes or until heated through.
Stir in 1 teaspoon rosewater, or to taste (see tip).
Pour into heatproof glasses; dust with ground cinnamon.

*tip The strength of rosewater varies from
brand to brand, start with a little less,
then taste and adjust to your liking.*

SALTED CAROB LATTE

PREP + COOK TIME **10 MINUTES**
SERVES **2 (MAKES 3 CUPS)**

Split a vanilla bean lengthways, scrape seeds from one
pod half using the tip of a knife; add seeds and pod half
to a small saucepan. Add 3 cups soy milk, 1½ tablespoons
carob powder, pinch of salt flakes and 1 tablespoon raw
honey to pan. Place pan over low-medium heat; simmer,
stirring continuously, for 5 minutes or until carob powder
dissolves and mixture is heated. Discard pod. Transfer to
a blender; blend until frothy. Pour into heatproof glasses;
dust with ¼ teaspoon carob powder.

*tip Carob powder is a natural, caffeine-free
alternative to cocoa powder. It is available
from health food stores and online.*

SLEEP WELL

VEGAN LATTE

KUMARA & COCONUT
TARTS WITH PECAN PRALINE

PREP + COOK TIME **45 MINUTES (+ COOLING & REFRIGERATION)** SERVES **6**

1½ CUPS (180G) GROUND ALMONDS

⅓ CUP (50G) COCONUT FLOUR

2 TABLESPOONS TAPIOCA FLOUR

2 TABLESPOONS COCONUT SUGAR

1 TEASPOON GROUND GINGER

2 FREE-RANGE EGGS

⅓ CUP (80G) COCONUT OIL, MELTED

500G (1 POUND) KUMARA (ORANGE SWEET POTATO), CUT INTO 3CM (1¼-INCH) PIECES

1 TABLESPOON WATER

¾ CUP (180ML) COCONUT CREAM

2 FREE-RANGE EGGS, EXTRA

¼ CUP (60ML) PURE MAPLE SYRUP

1 TEASPOON MIXED SPICE

1 CUP (280G) COCONUT YOGHURT

PECAN PRALINE

¾ CUP (90G) PECAN HALVES

½ CUP (80G) COCONUT SUGAR

½ CUP (125ML) WATER

1 Preheat oven to 180°C/350°F. Grease six 10cm (4-inch) round flan tins with removable bases.

2 Process ground almonds, flours, coconut sugar and ginger in a food processor to combine. Add eggs and coconut oil, processing until just combined. Press mixture evenly over base and side of tins. Place tins on an oven tray.

3 Bake tart shells for 10 minutes or until golden.

4 Meanwhile, place kumara and the water in a small microwave-safe bowl; cover with plastic wrap. Microwave on High (100%) for 8 minutes or until tender. Drain; cool.

5 Blend or process kumara with coconut cream, extra eggs, maple syrup and mixed spice until smooth. Pour mixture into tart shells.

6 Bake tarts for 15 minutes until just set with a slight wobble in the centre. Turn oven off; cool in oven. Refrigerate for 2 hours.

7 Make pecan praline.

8 Just before serving, top tarts with yoghurt and praline.

pecan praline Spread nuts on a baking-paper-lined oven tray. Stir coconut sugar and the water in a small saucepan over medium-high heat, without boiling, until sugar dissolves. Bring to the boil; boil, uncovered, without stirring, for 6 minutes until it reaches hard crack stage (when a drizzle of syrup dropped into iced water turns into hard brittle shards). Pour toffee over nuts on tray, titling to spread into a thin even layer. Allow to cool and set. Break praline into pieces.

nutritional count per serving
51.5g total fat (21.5g saturated fat); 3282kJ (784 cal); 62.1g carbohydrate; 18.4g protein; 9.7g fibre

tip Tarts can be made up to 2 days ahead; store, covered in the fridge. Just before serving, top with yoghurt and praline.

RASPBERRY RIPPLE
SWEET CORN
ICE-CREAM

PREP + COOK TIME **1 HOUR 30 MINUTES (+ STANDING & FREEZING)** SERVES **8**

This healthy non-dairy ice-cream is made with corn, which provides a natural creaminess and sweetness. Expect the ice-cream to be slightly more icy as a result.

2 TRIMMED CORN COBS (500G)
2¼ CUPS (560ML) COCONUT CREAM
2 CUPS (500ML) UNSWEETENED ALMOND MILK
¼ CUP (55G) CASTER SUGAR (SUPERFINE SUGAR)
2 TEASPOONS VANILLA EXTRACT
½ CUP (125ML) AGAVE SYRUP
1½ CUPS (225G) FRESH OR THAWED FROZEN RASPBERRIES
CORNFLAKE CRUNCH
2 TABLESPOONS CASTER SUGAR (SUPERFINE SUGAR)
1 TABLESPOON AGAVE SYRUP
1 TABLESPOON OLIVE OIL
½ TEASPOON VANILLA EXTRACT
2 CUPS (80G) CORNFLAKES

1 Using a sharp knife, cut kernels from cobs; reserve cobs. Place corn kernels, cobs, coconut cream, almond milk and sugar in a large saucepan over medium-high heat; bring to the boil. Reduce heat; simmer for 5 minutes or until corn is tender. Stand for 1 hour.
2 Discard corn cobs. Blend or process corn mixture until smooth. Strain corn mixture; discard solids. Stir in extract and ⅓ cup of the agave syrup until combined.
3 Transfer corn mixture to an ice-cream machine. Churn mixture following manufacturer's instructions.
4 Meanwhile, blend or process raspberries with remaining agave syrup until smooth. Swirl raspberry mixture through almost frozen ice-cream to create a ripple effect; pour into a 1 litre (4 cup) freezer-proof container. Freeze overnight or until firm.
5 Make cornflake crunch.
6 Serve ice-cream topped with cornflake crunch.

cornflake crunch Preheat oven to 150°C/300°F. Line an oven tray with baking paper. Place sugar, agave syrup, oil and extract in a small saucepan over low heat, stirring, until sugar dissolves. Place cornflakes in a medium bowl. Add syrup mixture; stir to combine. Spread cornflake mixture on tray. Bake for 25 minutes or until slightly more golden. Leave on tray to cool. Break into small pieces.

nutritional count per serving
23g total fat (12.8g saturated fat); 1868kJ (447 cal); 52.3g carbohydrate; 6.2g protein; 5.2g fibre

tips Take the ice-cream out of the freezer 15 to 30 minutes before serving to allow it to soften slightly. If you like, you could freeze the ice-cream mixture in ice-block moulds; just before serving, coat them in cornflake crunch.

GLOSSARY

AGAVE SYRUP from the agave plant; has a low GI, but that is due to the high percentage of fructose present, which may be harmful in large quantities.

ALLSPICE also known as pimento or jamaican pepper; so-named because it tastes like a combination of nutmeg, cumin, clove and cinnamon. Available whole or ground.

ALMONDS

blanched brown skins removed.

flaked paper-thin slices.

ground also called almond meal.

BAKING PAPER also called parchment paper or baking parchmen; a silicone-coated paper used for lining baking pans and oven trays so cooked food doesn't stick, making removal easy.

BAKING POWDER a raising agent consisting mainly of two parts cream of tartar to one part bicarbonate of soda (baking soda).

BARLEY a nutritious grain used in soups and stews. Hulled barley, the least processed, is high in fibre. Pearl barley has had the husk removed then been steamed and polished so that only the 'pearl' of the original grain remains, much the same as white rice.

BEANS

broad (fava) available dried, fresh, canned and frozen. Fresh should be peeled twice (discarding both the outer long green pod and the beige-green tough inner shell); the frozen beans have had their pods removed but the beige shell still needs removal.

butter cans labelled butter beans are, in fact, cannellini beans. Confusingly, it's also another name for lima beans, sold both dried and canned; a large beige bean with a mealy texture and mild taste.

cannellini a small white bean similar in appearance and flavour to other white beans (great northern, navy or haricot), all of which can be substituted for the other. Available dried or canned.

kidney medium-sized red bean, slightly floury in texture, yet sweet in flavour.

white a generic term we use for canned or dried cannellini, haricot, navy or great northern beans belonging to the same family, *phaseolus vulgaris*.

BEETROOT (BEETS) firm, round root vegetable.

BICARBONATE OF SODA (BAKING SODA) a raising agent.

BLOOD ORANGE a virtually seedless citrus fruit with blood-red-streaked rind and flesh; sweet, non-acidic, salmon-coloured pulp and juice having slight strawberry or raspberry overtones. The rind is not as bitter as a regular orange.

BREADCRUMBS

panko (japanese) available as larger pieces and fine crumbs; have a lighter texture than Western-style crumbs. Available from most supermarkets.

packaged prepared fine-textured but crunchy white breadcrumbs; good for coating foods that are to be fried.

stale crumbs made by grating or processing 1- or 2-day-old bread.

BROCCOLINI a cross between broccoli and chinese kale; it has long asparagus-like stems with a long loose floret, both are edible. Resembles broccoli but is milder and sweeter in taste.

BRUISE a cooking term to describe the slight crushing given to aromatic ingredients, such as lemon grass and cardamom pods, with the flat side of a heavy knife to release flavour and aroma.

BUTTER use salted or unsalted (sweet) butter; 125g (4 ounces) is equal to one stick of butter.

CAPERS grey-green buds of a warm climate shrub (usually Mediterranean), sold either dried and salted or pickled in a vinegar brine. Capers must be rinsed well before using.

CAPSICUM (BELL PEPPER) also called pepper. Comes in many colours: red, green, yellow, orange and purplish-black. Be sure to discard seeds and membranes before use.

CARDAMOM a spice native to India and used extensively in its cuisine; can be purchased in pod, seed or ground form. Has a distinctive aromatic, sweetly rich flavour.

CHEESE

fetta Greek in origin; a crumbly textured goat- or sheep-milk cheese having a sharp, salty taste. Ripened and stored in salted whey.

fetta, persian a soft, creamy fetta marinated in a blend of olive oil, garlic, herbs and spices; available from most major supermarkets.

goat's made from goat's milk, has an earthy, strong taste; available in soft and firm textures, various shapes and sizes, and sometimes rolled in ash or herbs.

haloumi a firm, cream-coloured sheep-milk cheese matured in brine; haloumi can be grilled or fried, briefly, without breaking down. Should be eaten while still warm as it becomes tough and rubbery on cooling.

parmesan also called parmigiano; is a hard, grainy cow-milk cheese originating in Italy. Reggiano is the best variety.

ricotta a soft, sweet, moist, white cow-milk cheese with a low fat content and a slightly grainy texture. The name roughly translates as 'cooked again' and refers to ricotta's manufacture from a whey that is itself a by-product of other cheese making.

CHERVIL also called cicily; mildly fennel-flavoured member of the parsley family with curly dark-green leaves. Available fresh and dried but, like all herbs, is best used fresh; like coriander and parsley, its delicate flavour diminishes the longer it's cooked.

CHIA SEEDS contain protein and all the essential amino acids, as well as being fibre-rich and a wealth of vitamins, minerals and antioxidants.

CHICKPEAS (GARBANZO BEANS) an irregularly round, sandy-coloured legume. Has a firm texture even after cooking, a floury mouth-feel and robust nutty flavour; available canned or dried (soak for several hours in cold water before use).

CHILLI generally, the smaller the chilli, the hotter it is. Use rubber gloves when seeding and chopping fresh chillies as they can burn your skin. Removing seeds and membranes lessens the heat.

CHOCOLATE, DARK (SEMI-SWEET) also called luxury chocolate; made of a high percentage of cocoa liquor and cocoa butter, and little added sugar.

CINNAMON available in pieces (sticks or quills) and ground into powder; one of the world's most common spices.

COCOA POWDER also known as unsweetened cocoa; cocoa beans (cacao seeds) that have been fermented, roasted, shelled, ground into powder then cleared of most of the fat content.

dutch-processed is treated with an alkali to neutralise its acids. It has a reddish-brown colour, a mild flavour and easily dissolves in liquids.

COCONUT

cream obtained commercially from the first pressing of the coconut flesh alone, without the addition of water; the second pressing (less rich) is sold as coconut milk. Available in cans and cartons at most supermarkets.

desiccated concentrated, dried, unsweetened and finely shredded coconut flesh.

flaked dried flaked coconut flesh.

milk not the liquid inside (coconut water), but the diluted liquid from the second pressing of the white flesh of a mature coconut. Available in cans and cartons at most supermarkets.

oil is extracted from the coconut flesh, so you don't get any of the fibre, protein or carbohydrates present in the whole coconut. The best quality is virgin coconut oil, which is the oil pressed from the dried coconut flesh, and doesn't include the use of solvents or other refining processes.

shredded thin strips of dried coconut.

sugar see Sugar

CORIANDER (CILANTRO) also known as pak chee or chinese parsley; a bright-green leafy herb with a pungent flavour. Both stems and roots of coriander are also used in cooking; wash well before using. Also available ground or as seeds; these should not be substituted for fresh as the tastes are completely different.

CORNFLOUR (CORNSTARCH) available made from corn or wheat; used as a thickening agent in cooking.

COUSCOUS a fine, dehydrated, grain-like cereal product made from semolina; it swells to three or four times its original size when liquid is added. It is eaten like rice with a tagine, as a side dish or salad ingredient.

CREAM

pouring also called pure or fresh cream. It has no additives and contains a minimum fat content of 35%.

thickened (heavy) a whipping cream that contains a thickener. It has a minimum fat content of 35%.

CUMIN also known as zeera or comino; has a spicy, nutty flavour.

DUKKAH an Egyptian specialty spice mixture made up of roasted nuts, seeds and an array of aromatic spices.

EDAMAME (shelled soy beans) available frozen from Asian food stores and some supermarkets.

EGGPLANT also called aubergine. Ranging in size from tiny to very large and in colour from pale green to deep purple. Also available char-grilled in jars.

FENNEL also called finocchio or anise; a white to very pale green-white, firm, crisp, roundish vegetable. The bulb has a slightly sweet, anise flavour but the leaves have a much stronger taste.

FISH SAUCE also called nam pla or nuoc nam; made from pulverised salted fermented fish, most often anchovies. Has a pungent smell and strong taste, so use sparingly.

FLOUR

chickpea (besan) creamy yellow flour made from chickpeas; is very nutritious.

gluten-free plain (all-purpose) a blend of gluten-free flours and starches (may include corn, potato, tapioca, chickpea and rice flours).

plain (all-purpose) a general all-purpose wheat flour.

potato made from cooked, dehydrated and ground potato; not to be confused with potato starch which is made from potato starch only. Potato flour has a strong potato flavour and is a heavy flour, so a little goes a long way.

rice very fine, almost powdery, gluten-free flour; made from ground white rice.

self-raising plain flour sifted with baking powder in the proportion of 1 cup flour to 2 teaspoons baking powder.

tapioca a soft, fine, light white flour made from the root of the cassava plant.

wholemeal also known as wholewheat flour; milled with the wheat germ so is higher in fibre and more nutritional than plain flour.

FREEKEH is cracked roasted green wheat; available in health food, specialty food stores some larger supermarkets.

GAI LAN also called chinese broccoli, gai larn, gai lum and chinese kale; used more for its stems than its coarse leaves.

GINGER

fresh also called green or root ginger; thick gnarled root of a tropical plant.

ground also called powdered ginger; used as a flavouring in baking but cannot be substituted for fresh ginger.

GOJI BERRIES like most berries, goji berries are are rich in antioxidants, high in fibre, and are a stand out for their vitamins A and C, and iron content.

GOLDEN SYRUP a by-product of refined sugarcane; pure maple syrup or honey can be substituted. Treacle is more viscous, and has a stronger flavour and aroma than golden syrup.

HARISSA a Moroccan paste made from dried chillies, cumin, garlic, oil and caraway seeds. Available from Middle Eastern food shops and supermarkets.

KAFFIR LIME LEAVES aromatic leaves of a citrus tree; two glossy dark green leaves joined end to end, forming a rounded hourglass shape. A strip of fresh lime peel may be substituted for each kaffir lime leaf.

KUMARA (ORANGE SWEET POTATO) the Polynesian name of an orange-fleshed sweet potato often confused with yam.

LEMON GRASS a tall, clumping, lemon-smelling and -tasting, sharp-edged grass; the white part of the stem is used, finely chopped, in cooking.

LENTILS (red, brown, yellow) dried pulses often identified by and named after their colour; also known as dhal.

LSA A ground mixture of linseeds (L), sunflower seeds (S) and almonds (A); available from supermarkets and health food stores.

MAPLE SYRUP, PURE distilled from the sap of sugar maple trees found only in Canada and the USA. Maple-flavoured syrup or pancake syrup is not an adequate substitute for the real thing.

MIRIN a Japanese champagne-coloured cooking wine; made of glutinous rice and alcohol and used expressly for cooking. Not to be confused with sake.

MIXED SPICE a classic spice mixture generally containing caraway, allspice, coriander, cumin, nutmeg and ginger, although cinnamon and other spices can be added.

MUSHROOMS

enoki clumps of long, spaghetti-like stems with tiny, snowy white caps.

oyster also called abalone; grey-white mushrooms shaped like a fan. Prized for their smooth texture and subtle, oyster-like flavour. Also available pink.

porcini also called cèpes; the richest-flavoured mushrooms. Expensive, but because they're so strongly flavoured, only a small amount is required.

shiitake, fresh also known as chinese black, forest or golden oak mushrooms; although cultivated, they are large and meaty and have the earthiness and taste of wild mushrooms.

swiss brown also calledcremini or roman mushrooms; are light brown mushrooms with a full-bodied flavour.

NORBU (MONK FRUIT SUGAR) monk fruit is a subtropical melon that contains a group of sweet tasting antioxidant compounds. Used as an alternative to cane sugar, as it has 96% fewer kilojoules and will not affect blood glucose or insulin levels.

NORI a type of dried seaweed used in Japanese cooking as a flavouring, garnish or for sushi. Sold in thin sheets, plain or toasted (yaki-nori).

OIL

coconut see Coconut

olive made from ripened olives. Extra virgin and virgin are the first and second press, respectively, of the olives; "light" refers to taste not fat levels.

peanut pressed from ground peanuts; most commonly used oil in Asian cooking because of its high smoke point (capacity to handle high heat without burning).

sesame made from roasted, crushed, white sesame seeds; used as a flavouring rather than a cooking oil.

vegetable sourced from plant fats.

ONION

green (scallions) also called, incorrectly, shallot; an immature onion picked before the bulb has formed. Has a long, bright-green edible stalk.

shallots also called french or golden shallots or eschalots; small and brown-skinned.

ORANGE BLOSSOM WATER concentrated flavouring made from orange blossoms.

PEPITAS (PUMPKIN SEEDS) are the pale green kernels of dried pumpkin seeds; they are available plain or salted.

PERSIMMONS an autumnal fruit available in two varieties: an stringent one, eaten soft, and a non-astringent, or sweet, variety also known as fuji fruit.

POLENTA a flour-like cereal made of ground corn (maize). Also the name of the dish made from it.

POMEGRANATE dark-red, leathery-skinned fruit about the size of an orange filled with hundreds of seeds, each wrapped in an edible lucent-crimson pulp with a unique tangy sweet-sour flavour.

POMEGRANATE MOLASSES not to be confused with pomegranate syrup or grenadine; pomegranate molasses is thicker, browner and more concentrated in flavour – tart, sharp, slightly sweet and fruity. Available from Middle Eastern food stores or specialty food shops, and some supermarkets.

POPPY SEEDS small, dried, bluish-grey seeds of the poppy plant, with a crunchy texture and a nutty flavour. Can be purchased whole or ground in delicatessens and most supermarkets.

QUINCE yellow-skinned fruit with hard texture and astringent, tart taste; eaten cooked or as a preserve. Long, slow cooking makes the flesh a deep rose pink.

QUINOA pronounced keen-wa; is a gluten-free grain. It has a delicate, slightly nutty taste and chewy texture.

RADICCHIO a red-leafed Italian chicory with a refreshing bitter taste that's eaten raw and grilled. Comes in varieties named after their places of origin, such as round-headed Verona or long-headed Treviso.

RICE MALT SYRUP also called brown rice syrup or rice syrup; is made by cooking brown rice flour with enzymes to break down its starch into sugars from which the water is removed.

ROASTING/TOASTING desiccated coconut, pine nuts and sesame seeds roast more evenly if stirred over low heat in a heavy-based frying pan; their natural oils will help turn them golden brown. Remove from pan immediately. Nuts and dried coconut can be roasted in the oven to release their aromatic essential oils. Spread them evenly onto an oven tray then roast at 180°C/350°F for about 5 minutes.

ROCKET (ARUGULA) peppery green leaf eaten raw in salads or used in cooking. Baby rocket leaves are smaller and less peppery.

ROSEWATER extract made from crushed rose petals, called gulab in India; used for its aromatic quality in many sweetmeats and desserts.

SAFFRON available ground or in strands; imparts a yellow-orange colour to food once infused. The quality can vary greatly; the best is the most expensive spice in the world.

SILVER BEET also called swiss chard; mistakenly called spinach.

SOY SAUCE made from fermented soya beans. Several variations are available in most supermarkets and Asian food stores. We use japanese soy sauce unless stated otherwise.

SPINACH also called english spinach and, incorrectly, silver beet.

STAR ANISE dried star-shaped pod with an astringent aniseed flavour; used to flavour stocks and marinades. Available whole and ground, it is an essential ingredient in chinese five-spice.

SUGAR

brown very soft, finely granulated sugar retaining molasses for its characteristic colour and flavour.

caster (superfine) finely granulated table sugar.

coconut is not made from coconuts, but the sap of the blossoms of the coconut palm tree. The refined sap looks a little like raw or light brown sugar, and has a similar caramel flavour. It also has the same amount of kilojoules as regular white (granulated) sugar.

icing (confectioners') also called powdered sugar; pulverised granulated sugar crushed together with a small amount of cornflour (cornstarch).

palm also called nam tan pip, jaggery, jawa or gula melaka; made from the sap of the sugar palm tree. Light brown to black in colour and usually sold in rock-hard cakes; use brown sugar if not available.

white (granulated) coarse, granulated table sugar, also called crystal sugar.

SUMAC a purple-red, astringent spice ground from berries of Mediterranean shrubs; adds a tart, lemony flavour to food. Available from major supermarkets.

TAHINI a rich, sesame-seed paste, used in most Middle-Eastern cuisines, especially Lebanese, in dips and sauces.

TAMARI a thick, dark soy sauce made mainly from soya beans, but without the wheat used in most standard soy sauces.

TAMARIND the tamarind tree produces clusters of hairy brown pods, each of which is filled with seeds and a viscous pulp, that are dried and pressed into the blocks of tamarind found in Asian food shops. Gives a sweet-sour, slightly astringent taste to marinades, sauces and dressings.

TOFU also known as bean curd; an off-white, custard-like product made from the "milk" of crushed soybeans. Comes fresh as soft or firm, and processed as fried or pressed dried sheets. Fresh tofu can be refrigerated in water (changed daily) for up to 4 days.

TOMATO

canned whole peeled tomatoes in natural juices; available crushed, chopped or diced. Use undrained.

mixed medley contains a mix of grape, baby roma, Zebrino and cherry tomatoes. Each has a distinct shape, size and flavour with colours ranging from yellow, to red and brown with stripes.

paste triple-concentrated tomato puree use to flavour soups, stews and sauces.

roma (egg) these are smallish, ovel-shaped tomatoes used in Italian cooking or salads.

TURMERIC also called kamin; is a rhizome related to galangal and ginger. Must be grated or pounded to release its acrid aroma and pungent flavour. Known for the golden colour it imparts, fresh turmeric can be substituted with the more commonly found dried powder.

VANILLA

bean dried, long, thin pod from a tropical golden orchid; the minuscule black seeds inside the bean impart a luscious flavour in baking and desserts.

extract obtained from vanilla beans infused in water; a non-alcoholic version of essence.

paste made from vanilla beans and contains real seeds. Is highly concentrated: 1 teaspoon replaces a whole vanilla bean. Found in most supermarkets in the baking section.

WATERCRESS one of the cress family, a large group of peppery greens. Highly perishable, so must be used as soon as possible after purchase. It has an exceptionally high vitamin K content, which is great for eye health, and is an excellent source of calcium.

WOMBOK (NAPA CABBAGE) also known as peking or chinese cabbage. Elongated in shape with pale green, crinkly leaves.

XANTHAN GUM is a thickening agent produced by fermentation of, usually, corn sugar. When buying xanthan gum, ensure the packet states 'made from fermented corn sugar'. Found in the health-food section in larger supermarkets.

YEAST (dried and fresh), a raising agent used in dough making. Granular (7g sachets) and fresh compressed (20g blocks) yeast can almost always be substituted for the other.

YOGHURT we use plain full-cream yoghurt in our recipes.

greek-style plain yoghurt strained in a cloth (muslin) to remove the whey and to give it a creamy consistency.

ZUCCHINI also called courgette; small, pale- or dark-green or yellow vegetable. When young, its edible flowers can be stuffed and deep-fried.

CONVERSION CHART

MEASURES

One Australian metric measuring cup holds approximately 250ml; one Australian metric tablespoon holds 20ml; one Australian metric teaspoon holds 5ml.

The difference between one country's measuring cups and another's is within a two- or three-teaspoon variance, and will not affect your cooking results.
North America, New Zealand and the United Kingdom use a 15ml tablespoon.

All cup and spoon measurements are level. The most accurate way of measuring dry ingredients is to weigh them. When measuring liquids, use a clear glass or plastic jug with the metric markings.

The imperial measurements used in these recipes are approximate only. Measurements for cake pans are approximate only. Using same-shaped cake pans of a similar size should not affect the outcome of your baking. We measure the inside top of the cake pan to determine sizes.

We use large eggs with an average weight of 60g.

DRY MEASURES

METRIC	IMPERIAL
15G	½OZ
30G	1OZ
60G	2OZ
90G	3OZ
125G	4OZ (¼LB)
155G	5OZ
185G	6OZ
220G	7OZ
250G	8OZ (½LB)
280G	9OZ
315G	10OZ
345G	11OZ
375G	12OZ (¾LB)
410G	13OZ
440G	14OZ
470G	15OZ
500G	16OZ (1LB)
750G	24OZ (1½LB)
1KG	32OZ (2LB)

LIQUID MEASURES

METRIC	IMPERIAL
30ML	1 FLUID OZ
60ML	2 FLUID OZ
100ML	3 FLUID OZ
125ML	4 FLUID OZ
150ML	5 FLUID OZ
190ML	6 FLUID OZ
250ML	8 FLUID OZ
300ML	10 FLUID OZ
500ML	16 FLUID OZ
600ML	20 FLUID OZ
1000ML (1 LITRE)	1¾ PINTS

LENGTH MEASURES

METRIC	IMPERIAL
3MM	⅛IN
6MM	¼IN
1CM	½IN
2CM	¾IN
2.5CM	1IN
5CM	2IN
6CM	2½IN
8CM	3IN
10CM	4IN
13CM	5IN
15CM	6IN
18CM	7IN
20CM	8IN
22CM	9IN
25CM	10IN
28CM	11IN
30CM	12IN (1FT)

OVEN TEMPERATURES

The oven temperatures in this book are for conventional ovens; if you have a fan-forced oven, decrease the temperature by 10-20 degrees.

	°C (CELSIUS)	°F (FAHRENHEIT)
VERY SLOW	120	250
SLOW	150	300
MODERATELY SLOW	160	325
MODERATE	180	350
MODERATELY HOT	200	400
HOT	220	425
VERY HOT	240	475

INDEX

Beauty treatments

FIRST PUBLISHED IN 2016 BY BAUER MEDIA BOOKS, AUSTRALIA.
THIS EDITION PUBLISHED IN 2018.
BAUER MEDIA BOOKS IS A DIVISION OF BAUER MEDIA PTY LTD.

BAUER MEDIA BOOKS

PUBLISHER
SALLY EAGLE

EDITORIAL & FOOD DIRECTOR
SOPHIA YOUNG

EDITORIAL DIRECTOR-AT-LARGE
PAMELA CLARK

ART DIRECTOR & DESIGNER
HANNAH BLACKMORE

MANAGING EDITOR
STEPHANIE KISTNER

RECIPE EDITOR
REBECCA MELI

OPERATIONS MANAGER
DAVID SCOTTO

COVER & MODEL PHOTOGRAPHY

PHOTOGRAPHER
JAMES MOFFATT

STYLIST
LUCY TWEED

PHOTOCHEF
ANGELA DEVLIN

WITH THANKS TO OUR MODELS

TRISTA & WILLOW PATRIS
LILY BOWMAN
LUCY & BEAU TWEED
KATJA HARDING-IRMER
XANTHE ROBERTS & EVIE LOCKHART
MARY & GABRIELLE TARCHICHI
IDA HEISKANEN
PEPPI & MEIKE PHIZACKLEA

PRINTED IN CHINA
BY LEO PAPER PRODUCTS LTD

A CATALOGUE RECORD FOR THIS BOOK
IS AVAILABLE FROM THE NATIONAL
LIBRARY OF AUSTRALIA.

ISBN: 9781742458687 (PAPERBACK)

© BAUER MEDIA PTY LIMITED 2016
ABN 18 053 273 546

PUBLISHED BY BAUER MEDIA BOOKS,
A DIVISION OF BAUER MEDIA PTY LTD,
54 PARK ST, SYDNEY; GPO BOX 4088,
SYDNEY, NSW 2001, AUSTRALIA
PH +61 2 9282 8618; FAX +61 2 9126 3702
WWW.AWWCOOKBOOKS.COM.AU

ORDER BOOKS
PHONE 136 116 (WITHIN AUSTRALIA)

OR ORDER ONLINE AT
WWW.AWWCOOKBOOKS.COM.AU

SEND RECIPE ENQUIRIES TO
RECIPEENQUIRIES@BAUER-MEDIA.COM.AU